Contents

AR

Changes to this edition

Newly added

Most highly recommended

What is Authentic Relating?

Authenticity is acting and speaking in alignment with our inner feelings, desires, and needs. **Authentic Relating (AR)** is the practice of bringing our truth into connection with others', so that we can weave a more rich and truthful human experience.

The **Authentic Relating Games** contained in this manual are an easy and fun way to introduce AR into daily life. They can help us experience deeper connections, boost empathy, see the world through others' eyes, and understand ourselves better so that we can enjoy life more.

By the end of a game, you may feel like you've known your partner(s) for a long time. Many people express entering a room full of strangers and leaving feeling like lifelong friends. Every game is a unique experience, whether you are playing it for the first time or the hundredth, because there is something new to learn about others and ourselves every time we enter into a new connection.

From simple curiosity games, to awareness-building and group activities which can take individuals safely out of their comfort zone, Authentic Relating games have the ability to profoundly and positively impact how we interact and live.

This manual is the work of nine years (and counting). It contains a multitude of exercises, with the intention to increase presence, connection, self-awareness, and empathy in groups around the world. The "Games" contained here have been extensively play-tested by communities across the world. Thank you to **everyone who submitted a game!**

This work was compiled by Sara Ness of Authentic Revolution with editing by Jeannie Bogue, Ebony Phillips, and Ankati Day. Any games that use self-referential pronouns ("I", "me", "we") without attribution to a community refer to Sara and/or the Austin community. You can contact Sara at sara@authrev.com.

AR

How to Use This Manual

Pick a Game

All Games will create connection. Pick your game based on what you want yourself or others to experience.

· Want to stimulate conversation? Try a Curiosity game.
· Want to address a tension you haven't been able to speak to? Try a Feedback game.
· Want to spice up an event or party? Try a Self-Expression or Group Bonding game.

Games are organized by section based on how they tend to flow in an event. Usually we start with a Grounding game, move into a Group Bonding game, explore a theme with any of the other sections, use Energizing games whenever we need a pick-me-up, and end with some Appreciation. You can put together any flow you want, or just pick a game you like to play on its own.

Sara's most recommended Games are marked with double asterix **.

New games added with this edition are marked with a plus sign +

Play to Your Audience

Some Games will work well for people with no experience in body awareness, transformational work, or self-revealing. Others require basic physical and emotional awareness, the ability to own one's experience, or comfort with vulnerability. Choose with awareness of who you're working with, and make sure you demonstrate first whatever you ask others to do.

Do it Your Way

There are a hundred ways to play every game. You can try different timings, more playful or more serious ways of introduction, giving different examples, different group sizes, different wording on the instructions, different sentence stems. You can call it a "Game" or an "Exercise" or a "Magic Connection Experience". You can blindfold everybody, play in a park, or spring these on your family. Try different things and find what works for you!

If you're leading an Authentic Relating Games night, see the Creating Authentic Communities manual for suggestions on how to put together the flow of Games for a night.

Notes on the Format

Each Game has a listing for "Setup", "Time", "Instructions for Playing", "Variations" (where applicable), and "Attributions". Most of these are self-explanatory, but be aware that most games can be played in different-sized groups or with different timings. You may have to change some instructions if you change the basic format.

All times are approximate, and usually reflect how long I have experienced each game taking, with the inclusion of set-up and a few shares (where applicable).

Games will be attributed to their inventor(s) and home community wherever we know the source. Authentic Relating as a term, and the concept of Authentic Relating Games, come originally from Authentic World and the original manual compiled by Bryan Bayer and Decker Cunov.

If you notice an incomplete or incorrect attribution, please email me so I can correct it. If you find a modification to a game that you like, or invent a new one, submit it here for inclusion into the next version of the manual.

Further Resources

Visit www.authrev.org/facilitation-center for:

· Full Games Night plans
· Sentence Stems
· Sample community agreements
· Training videos
· AR-adjacent games
· A full lexicon
· ....and more!

AR

Key Words and Phrases

You'll see many of these mentioned throughout the manual, so here is a guide to some of the language we use in Authentic Relating.

Authentic Relating (AR)
A mode of communication that involves acknowledging and revealing one's own feelings, thoughts, motivations, and perceptions.

Circling
A relational meditation practice in which you speak your physical and emotional experience in this moment, with these people.

Context
The surroundings or frame of a statement, experience, or event, that may or may not change the meaning of it.

Check In
Confirm with either a group or an individual what is going on in that moment, or what has been happening for them, and how they are feeling now, or they need right now.
· "I just want to check in - how are we doing?"
· "Let's go around the circle and check in. Can everybody share how you are feeling right now?"

Dropped In
Feeling present in your own experience and grounded into yourself here, now.

Edgy
An experience that puts the person into a place of emotional discomfort, but not overwhelm.
· "I'm attracted to you, and it feels edgy to say that."

Facilitator
The person holding space for the group to create, participate and connect.

Feeling
Physical: A sensation. A somatic experience. Emotional: An emotion. Judgment: A common misuse of language.
Physical feeling: "My arms tingle and there is a sharp ache behind my forehead."
Emotional feeling: "I'm angry." "I'm a little scared and mostly excited."
Judgment: "I feel like you're not telling the truth right now."

Getting Someone's World
Taking the time to understand and/or embody someone else's perspective on reality.
· "Once I got her world around the conflict, I could understand why she was so angry with me!"

Hold Space
Fully and impartially listening to, being present with, and accepting somebody. An invitation for emotional openness.

Integral

A developmental theory about individual and collective human evolution, often used in association with Circling and Authentic Relating. Developed by philosopher Ken Wilber as a synthesis of psychological, philosophical, and religious theories across many cultures and modalities.

Owning Your Experience

Identifying the locus of responsibility for feelings, actions, thoughts, beliefs, judgments, and behaviors within oneself, and communicating this through language such as "I" statements.
· "You seem angry. I feel scared."

"Popcorn Style" Shares

Without guidance or taking explicit turns, letting people speak whenever they feel the desire to do so.
· "We're going to take shares popcorn style. Anybody can speak up when you have something to say."

Sentence Stems

Beginning fragments of a sentence to finish by one or all participants.

Shadow

A side you normally would rather not acknowledge of yourself.
· "My shadow is trying to please everyone around me. It makes people like me, but I tend to lose connection with what I'm actually feeling or what I want."

Sharebacks

Shares. I have no idea why the "backs" is in there.
· "Baby got share....backs!"

Shared Reality

Consensus on the world we're experiencing. "I know that you know that I know," etc. Most of the time we don't have this. Getting shared reality is core to Authentic Relating practice.
· "Do we have shared reality that "clean" means all the dishes are put away?"

(Sharing) Impact

Sharing with the group, or a specific person, verbally how you were affected by an event or statement.
· "You seem upset. Could you share the impact on you from what Sandra said?"

The Austin Love Juggernaut

The Austin Authentic Relating community.

Transpersonal

Creating or encouraging the awareness of something beyond our ordinary sense of self.

Triggered

Experiencing emotional intensity, usually negative/uncomfortable emotions (anger, pain, sadness, etc).
"I'm really triggered by what you just said. It reminds me of feeling left out of games when I was little."

Agreements

These are usually shared at the beginning of an Authentic Relating game night, so may not be needed for an informal context. However, they point to some of the core values of Authentic Relating, so are very useful for new people. Feel free to use some or all of these to help create a culture before playing some AR games.

1. RESPECT YOURSELF

You are your main priority. If you have bodily or emotional needs that are keeping you from being fully involved, please take care of those first. You are welcome to sit out of one or all of the Games. You can change your mind at any time. The more you take responsibility for yourself, the more freedom you and others have to play without worrying about others' unspoken needs.

2. LEAN INTO YOUR EDGE

Authentic Relating Games are meant to take us places that we don't often go in everyday conversation. These games are an invitation to lean into the edge of discomfort that comes with true authenticity, in a space that's kept safe for vulnerability . . . as long as you do so while still respecting yourself. Find your own edge, and lean into new ways of sharing and being together. There is no one right way to do this.

3. STAY PRESENT

Remain aware of your own sensations, emotions, and needs during the games. Notice where your attention is. If it wanders away from yourself or your partner, gently bring your awareness back into connection. The more conscious you are of yourself, the more you will get out of this work.

4. CONFIDENTIALITY BY REQUEST

If you feel you've shared something you would like to remain private, ask for confidentiality from those you've shared it with. We use confidentiality by request - rather than blanket confidentiality - because it allows us to practice asking for what we need, and because vulnerable sharing can happen inside or outside of an explicit Games container. It's easier to remember a specific request than everything shared within a session.

5. CHECK YOUR ASSUMPTIONS

We make up stories about others, and the world, to filter the amount of social information we are receiving at any given moment. One of the most powerful tools in Authentic Relating is to check these assumptions. If somebody seems distant, angry, confused, joyful, angry, etc., checking in can help align your perception with reality, so that you can relate with the person rather than your story of who they are. This keeps us from saving those who seem uncomfortable, distancing from those who seem angry, etc. You can check your assumptions by saying, "Can I check an assumption about you? I imagine you're feeling/experiencing/wanting...."

Grounding
Games

Grounding Games

We all get told to "be present" and "keep our attention in the here and now". But despite the tips and the meditation courses, keeping our attention focused is hard, especially around other people. Social media and social anxiety train our minds to wander away. We need invitations to help bring them back.

Grounding games invite participants to notice what is happening both inside of and between them. As such, they promote self-awareness, self-regulation, focus, and the ability to notice subtlety. They set up the skills we need for any successful event.

Map of the Territory

· *Noting and Contexter* are games that, like meditation, draw our attention to what is happening

  inside of us, independent of the other person or people in the room.
· *Crowdsourced Meditation, Guided Presence, Feng Shui, Frame,* and *Lens of Attention* offer
  the chance for the facilitator - or, in most of these, anyone in the room - to guide our attention
  towards something specific, and notice what changes inside.
· *Noticing, Handshake Game, See and Be Seen,* and *The Head and the Heart* move to a
  relational space, where we become aware of ourselves specifically within connection to others.

When to use Grounding Games:

· At the beginning of an event or session, to help participants arrive mentally as well as physically
· When there is a lot of emotion or intensity in the group, as a reset
· At any time in events focused around presence

Index

Noting

Setup
Pairs

Time
5-10 Minutes

Noting brings individuals into a quick, deep, meditative presence, especially if eye contact is kept all the way through.

Instructions for Playing

In pairs, come into presence with your partner, then choose an "A" and a "B". A's speak first. For 3 (or more) minutes, A will give a single word to anything that passes through their awareness, and speak it aloud. Words can be broad categories - "Thought. Sensation. Feeling. Thought. Thought." - or more specific: "Itch. Confusion. Questioning. Fear. Thought. Blankness." After 3 minutes are up, switch roles.

Variations

Relational Attention Awareness: Divide into pairs. Person A has 3 minutes to label, moment by moment, the location of their attention between 'self', 'other', or 'both'. Person B will silently witness. 'Self' is when one's attention is within their own experience; 'other' is when their attention is with their partner's experience; 'both' is when their attention is in between. Briefly share what that was like, then switch roles.

Attributions

Taken from a workshop by Micah Sutton of the Austin Love Juggernaut. Variation by Valerie Steen of Fort Collins Authentic Relating Group.

Contexter

The purpose of this game is to acclimate people to the terms "dropped in" and "connected" by noticing and presencing context. Also, it promotes self-awareness.

Instructions for Playing

Lead a connection to self/grounding meditation and request that as participants open their eyes, they bring that "connected" feeling out with them.

Then complete this sentence stem: "What's happening right now is…" Participants begin answering the sentence stem, popcorn-style, for about 3-5 minutes without any rebuttals from others (jazz fingers for resonance are okay).

Facilitator Instructions

Sporadically and randomly throughout the game, the facilitator can ask where the participants' "grounded"/ "dropped in"/ "connected" feeling is.

Attributions

Developed by Mike Blas of the Austin community.

**Crowdsourced Meditation

I rarely start out a night in Austin without some form of individual or group meditation. Self-awareness is a precursor to authenticity, and it helps people to land in the present moment. This game is a beautiful way to combine individual presence with group involvement. ~Sara Ness

Instructions for Playing

Participants all close their eyes and tune into their experience. Then, anytime someone feels called, they can name what they are aware of right now. For example, "My hands are sweating." "I feel nervous." "I'm taking deep breaths." Your experience may be influenced by what you hear, or it may stay the same - either is fine. Use others' awareness to guide you deeper into your own.

Facilitator Instructions

Start the sharing yourself, to give an example. Tell participants that it's okay if they speak at the same time or overlap.

Variations

· Guided Meditation: Anybody can offer a suggestion for what the group should pay attention to in the meditation, based on what they are aware of in the moment: "Become aware of your hands," "imagine that there is no ground beneath you," "take a breath and feel down into your chest," etc. Let suggestions flow naturally for 5-10 minutes.

Attributions

Sara Ness of the Austin Love Juggernaut

Guided Presence

Instructions for Playing

Mill around the room. Then find yourselves in front of somebody and make eye contact as you ponder the following noticing thoughts and questions (see facilitator instructions for example). Give shares afterward.

Facilitator Instructions

Read this out loud while participants are standing in front of each other making eye contact.

"Maybe you know this person, or maybe they are a stranger. Maybe you've got a story about who this person is. Either way, let it go. What's different about this connection? What's the same? Are you breathing? Where is your attention - on you, your partner, on both? Are you hearing any judgments in your head? (Just notice them and let them go). What is the flavor of this connection? Close your eyes. Inhale. Exhale. Do you have any expectations about what this connection should look like? Are you looking for validation from the person across from you? What do you see in this person's eyes that reminds you of yourself? What if this was your last 15 minutes on Earth? How might this interaction be different for you?"

Variations

· Contexted Connection: Participants keep moving, and make eye contact with each other in different ways - as though you're walking by somebody on the street, as if you're suspicious about the other people, as if you are feeling friendly towards others, to look at others in the way you think they'd like to be seen, etc. Give sharebacks afterwards: how did that feel in your body, or how trusting did you feel towards others, just by changing your context for how to see other people?

Attributions

Developed by Mike Blas of the Austin community.

+Feng Shui

Setup
Full group/small group (4-7 people)

Time
15-30 min

Feng Shui is a traditional Chinese practice, used to find the most harmonious orientation and layout of buildings and other structures. This game explores how different physical arrangements of people lend themselves to different emotional states.

Instructions for Playing

Sit in a circle. Take time for everyone to notice how they feel in this physical configuration, and then share what they notice popcorn-style with the group. Notice things like whether you feel connected or disconnected from the others, serious or playful, energetic or low-energy, etc.

After taking a few shares, change to a new configuration, e.g. a standing circle. Now, in standing, share what this new configuration feels like, and how it feels different from the previous configuration.

Continue changing configurations, and notice how each configuration feels different.

Facilitator Instructions

Prompt the configuration changes. Optionally, have participants call out new configurations for the group. This game is great in facilitator trainings as a way to give people a direct sense of how arranging the room can subtly shift people's experience.

Variations

Play with elements such as:
· Close or far apart
· Standing or sitting
· Facing each other or facing away
· Touching or not touching
· Everyone doing the same thing, or some participants arranged differently (e.g. one person standing while everyone else sits)

Attributions

Game created and submitted by Jesse Reilly from Brisbane Authentics

**"Frame"

This is like the Noticing game, but by saying the word "Frame," helps create a snapshot or a still-life of the moment to be admired, appreciated, and noticed.

Instructions for Playing

In pairs, go back and forth. First person says, "Frame"... then makes a statement about what they notice in the moment. Imagine that this moment of human contact is like a precious piece of art that you have just framed, and then, like a connoisseur, describe the moment in a short phrase or statement to their partner. The other partner repeats, starting again with "Frame." Repeat as desired, or mix and match different partners.

Facilitator Instructions

At the end, offer a sentence stem, or a moment for feedback.
This game can also be played in small groups.

Attributions

Submitted by Daniel Johnson of Authentic Relating Philadelphia ,
who said it comes from the early days of Authentic SF.

Lens of
Attention

Have fun with this and be creative with the topics. There is no limit to how long to stay on any given focus of attention.

Instructions for Playing

In a group, answer the sentence stem "When I put my attention on…, I notice…" The game leader will choose an object of attention for the first few rounds. For example, "Put your attention on your breath". Participants then go around, "When I put my attention on my breath, I notice….." Do 2-4 rounds of this. Breath, Body, Heart, Emotions, Desire, the Group, the Connection, etc.

Then, someone else chooses. Any participant at any time can change the lens of attention to anything. A change is initiated with, "Let's put our attention on…" Then, everyone shares what they notice as they place their attention on that thing.

Example:
· "Let's put our attention on Jessica."
· "When I put my attention on Jessica, I notice your smile."
· "…I notice joy."
· "…I notice a gentleness."
· "Let's put our attention on gentleness."
· "When I put my attention on gentleness, I notice that I start judging myself for not being gentle."
· "I notice feeling safe."

You can stay for a few minutes, or half an hour, or you can immediately jump to a different focus of attention if you don't like the suggestion.

Put your attention on Cotton Candy, or the infinite mystery of life, or childhood memories, or conflict, etc. If anyone is struggling to focus their attention, it's also fine to say: "When I put my attention on the connection in this group, I notice that I don't want to put my attention on connection." Or… "I notice that it's very difficult for me to focus my attention." Everything can be included.

Attributions

Invented by Daniel Johnson.

**Noticing

Setup
Pairs

Time
5-30 min

"Noticing" is the granddaddy of them all - the best way I know of to draw people into a conversation about connection rather than content, and a perfect game for any situation, including social events, bars, and parties.

Instructions for Playing

In pairs choose who will go first - participant A or B.
A begins: "Sitting/standing here with you, I notice . . ." identifying something in their experience of the moment.
B responds, "Hearing that, I notice . . ."
Go back and forth: "Hearing that, I notice . . . Hearing that, I notice . . ." for 2-5 minutes.

B's noticing does not have to be directly influenced by what A notices; the wording is meant to acknowledge relationship, but what's most important is awareness of one's self in the moment.

Facilitator Instructions

Direct participants' attention to notice their feelings, sensations, and emotions. In this they can notice everything, even the things they choose to not share. The intention of this game is to have people pay attention to what's happening inside them while they are with others.

Variations

· Bodily Sensations: "Being with you, I feel..." some physical feeling in one's own body, without interpretation

· Feelings: "Being with you, I feel..." some emotion in one's own body, without interpretations. Can be combined with bodily sensations.

· Feelings, "Because": "Being with you, I feel...because..." Each person gives a "headline" for the cause (or causes) behind their feeling. Notice how being given context changes our experience of the other.

· Thoughts: "Being with you, I'm thinking...",

· Things About the Other: "Being with you, I notice…" a thing about the other person that can be directly observed, e.g. being with you I notice the length of your hair. Steer away from interpretation or imagination; see how unarguable your observations can be.

· Notice and Imagine: "Being with you, I notice [something directly observable about the other], and I imagine…" Optional: speaker checks in with person B, "Is that true?" and let B share what's more true for them in the moment.

· Notice, Imagine, Feel, Desire: Go back and forth, saying "I notice [something directly observable about the other]…I imagine…I feel…and I want…". It's ok if you miss some of the pieces.

· Curious Noticing: Partner A has 2-3 minutes to speak about the curiosities they have about partner B. Switch. This can also be played as an exchange, with A: "I'm curious about…" and B: "Hearing that, I'm curious about…"

· Connection Appreciation: In groups of 3-4. For each group, 2 people play all out noticing for 90 seconds, with the other/others in the group witnessing the connection. After noticing, all three (or four) people share about the connection that just happened between the pair. Continue until all three (or six) pair combinations are done. Then the full group shares about the experience.

· Group Noticing: The Facilitator or person of choice, offers a sentence stem, "While I sit here, I feel . . . " or "While I sit here, I think . . . " or "While I sit here, I notice . . . ". Specify bodily sensations, emotions, thoughts, or all-out noticing. Participants go around in a circle, each completing the stem in one sentence or less. Try not to think of what you're going to say while others are sharing, and to notice the impact that each person's share has on you.

· Gossip Noticing: Get into pairs around a circle. First, notice physical things about the other pairs in the room. Gestures, clothes, facial expressions. Talk about this to your partner for 3 minutes. Then, for two minutes, practice emotional noticings of others around the room. What are they feeling? What are your imaginings of them or their connection as a pair? Lastly, let your imagination run wild. Project onto those around the room. What's their relationship to each other? What context might they do well together? Are they in a movie? Who are they? Discuss this for 3 minutes. Allow for full group debrief.

Attributions

The original Noticing game was brought into the
Authentic communities by Guy Sengstock or Decker Cunov.
"Curious Noticing" and "Feelings, Because…" come from Mike Blas; "Connection Appreciation" comes from Chad Phillips; Gossip Noticing from Zachary Robison.

**Handshake Game

This is a great game for groups to meet each other at the beginning of a night, to validate connections at the end, or to drop back into relational space at any point during an event.

Instructions for Playing

Find a partner to stand in front of and make non-verbal eye contact.

When one person feels that they have "met" the other (or feels present with them - your choice of prompt), they put out their hand to shake. When the other also feels present or met, he/she should shake the hand. Then, each partner moves to another unoccupied person.

If you've met everybody, take a seat and continue practicing nonverbal presence with self or eye contact with other seated people. Continue until each person has "met" everybody else in the room. Then give shares.

Facilitator Instructions

Prompt participants that they should not put out their hand just because their partner has, but to wait until they feel satisfied before extending their own to shake.

In larger groups, you may want to time the game and let participants know that they will not meet everybody there. Since this is a nonverbal game, you may want to have at least one facilitator out to make sure people can signal if they're not feeling safe.

Variations

· Heartshake: A and B each put their left hand on the other's heart, and cover the other person's left hand with their own free hand. (B's left hand is on A's chest, covered by A's right hand, and vice versa.)

  Partners take 3 breaths together. Then, they hug for 3 breaths. Separate and find a new partner.
  Works best with music playing.

Attributions

Handshake was invented by the Austin Love Juggernaut.
Heartshake comes from the Integral Center

**See and Be Seen

Setup
Full group

Time
5-10 min

This game is a beautiful and simple way to become aware of the felt shift in attention when focusing on self, other, or the space between. It is surprisingly insightful and vulnerable.

Instructions for Playing

Mill around the room and then stop in front of a partner and close your eyes. When you open them, the person with shorter hair is silently "seeing" and the other is "being seen". Close your eyes and come back to self. Open eyes and switch roles, still without speaking.

Close your eyes and come back to self. Open eyes and both see and be seen at the same time. Then, thank your partner nonverbally and move on.

Facilitator Instructions

Ideally, follow this up with another pair exercise.

Variations

· Appreciative Sight: The person "seeing" notices the other with deep appreciation, noticing how much they can enjoy this person's physical appearance or way of being. The person being "seen" feels what it's like to be so deeply appreciated, without having to do anything to deserve it. This version can also be played as a Spotlight game, with one person being "seen" and accepted by the group for 4-6 minutes.

Attributions

I experienced this exercise in an immersion led by John and Sean of Circling Europe, but have also seen it in workshops with the Circling Institute.

The Head and the Heart

Setup
Full Group / Pairs

Time
10 minutes

Instructions for Playing

Everyone mills around the room, each person tuning in to the conversation going on in their own head - noticing the pace of it, the volume of it, the contents of it. Participants can notice others in the space, but stay within your own experience and do not make eye contact at first.

Eventually, everyone starts finding others' eyes as they walk around the space. Then, come to stand in front of a partner, and after a moment of silent eye contact, participants share the sentence stem, "Something my head is saying right now is..." Once both partners have shared, make a sign of acknowledgement and begin milling about the room again. Repeat with several new partners.

After a few rounds, come to silence wherever you are, close your eyes, and see if you can drop your awareness a bit lower, down into the heart. Feel into your own body and notice which parts you feel the most.

Open your eyes and walk around again with this new awareness, tuned into the heart-space (which may mean something different for everyone).

Eventually, start making eye contact with others in the space, and come to stand facing a new partner. After a moment of silence, each partner will complete the sentence stem, "Something my heart is saying right now is..." Then thank each other and repeat a few times with new partners.

Notes

This game was created by Shaina List of Authentic Relating Toronto.

Energizing
Games

Energizing Games

Let's face it, life can be boring. But events don't have to be. Even if you're going for the deepest possible experience of self-awareness and collective transformation, you'll still need an outlet for play, joy, and the natural heebie-jeebies that the body is heir to.

Energizing Games are a mix of improv comedy exercises and movement games that, when done right, get participants out of their heads and into their spontaneity. Make sure that you participate in these as well as lead them, since your willingness to lean in will spark participants as well.

Map of the Territory

- Rock Paper Scissors Tournament, In Groups of..., and Best Friends/Mortal Enemies are fun games that get participants up and moving.
- "I'm a Tree", How's Yours, and Fortune Cookie are minimally challenging improv games that get participants to collaborate on creating a sentence or scene.
- Whatcha Doin', Bumblebee, Getting Presents, Word Association, and I Love Myself! are faster-moving games that require participants to act or speak without overthinking.

When to use Energizing Games:

- At the beginning of an event or session
- After breaks or meals
- When the group seems stuck or heavy, to create movement and creativity

Index

- *Rock Paper Scissors Tournament
- In Groups of....
- Best Friends /Mortal Enemies
- *I'm a Tree!
- "How's Yours?"
- *Fortune Cookie

- *Whatcha Doin'?
- Bumblebee
- +Conductor
- *+Getting Presents
- Word Association
- I Love Myself

**Rock Paper Scissors Tournament

Setup
Full Group

Time
5-10 Minutes

This game is a great way to warm up any kind of group.

Instructions for Playing

Play "Rock, Paper, Scissors" in pairs. The loser stands behind the winner and follows them around, cheering and chanting for them to win at other bouts. If the winner loses, they and everybody behind them goes to stand behind and cheer for the new winner. Eventually everybody will be behind one person after the last round is won, and then the winner can take a victory lap!

Facilitator Instructions

Play as many rounds as everyone is having fun with.

Attributions

A variation on an old classic

In Groups Of....

Setup
Full Group /
Breakout Groups

Time
10 Minutes

A great warm up to use just for fun and for everyone to get in their bodies, in the room, and interacting.

It can also be an opportunity for people to explore and observe how they interact with others - Are you: Active about finding a group? Passive about being found for a group?
Do you become the leader in making a group? Active in leading with ideas of how to execute, following, using words more or just getting in there and doing it and letting others respond. ~ Amy Silverman

Instructions for Playing

Play this as best you can without worrying about being exact. Just "do it".
Participants scramble into groups and work together to create a human form version of an item the facilitator calls out (examples below).

Facilitator Instructions

Call out "In Groups Of... (number of people) make a _____" (car, human body, crane, computer, house, wedding set, swing set, airplane, etc). After a brief time (20-40 seconds), count down 5,4,3,2,1, which signals them to complete and settle into their positions. The facilitator can have fun commenting on anything that stands out, or tell everyone to hold their positions and check out a particularly creative or funny group or two. Then continue on to the next command "In Groups Of... make a _____".

A great way to bring everyone together afterwards is to say "In Group of 25 (or however many people you approximately have in attendance) make a circle" and everyone circles-up for debrief or whatever you're doing next.

Attributions

Amy Silverman of The Connection Movement NY.

Best Friends / Mortal Enemies

Setup
Full Group

Time
5-10 Minutes

Instructions for Playing

Mill around the room. Then nonverbally, (without giving it away!) choose somebody to be your "best friend". On the count of three, get as close as possible to your "friend".

Have the group scatter and mingle again. Now, each person choose a "mortal enemy". On the count of three, get as far away as possible from your "enemy".

In the final round, try to get your "friend" between you and your "enemy".

Facilitator Instructions

Encourage that people should keep moving, especially in the last round, to make sure that they are at the maximum closeness or distance from their BF/ME.

Also remind them that this does not have to be your real best friend or mortal enemy (though it CAN be...)

Attributions

I experienced this game at an Integral Center event. Warning - laughter may ensue.

Race Cars

Setup
Pairs

Time
7-10 min

This game is a very fun icebreaker that gets even the most heady of people into their bodies, especially if the theme is something having to do with trust or support. ~Dan Sieling

Instructions for Playing

One partner (A) closes their eyes while the other partner ("B") stands behind them, and puts their hands on A's shoulders. A begins to walk forward, while B guides A (hopefully) making sure not to let A bump into anyone/anything.

After a minute, the facilitator guides each pair to go a little faster (or "2nd gear" if you really want to ham up the race car metaphor) for a bit, and a little faster (or "3rd gear"), and so on until everyone is practically running around the room.

The facilitator can guide the group to speed up, slow down, or stop, as he/she pleases. Then slowly come to a stop. B drivers close their eyes, and the A race cars then pick new partners, so that Bs don't know who picked them.

Facilitator Instructions

Another option is to switch drivers mid-round, which can add a fun twist to the game as well.

Attributions

Contributed by Dan Sieling of The Connection Movement NY,
who discovered it at Authentic World's T3 training and again at an Acroyoga immersion.

**"I'm a Tree!"

Setup
Full Group or Triads

Time
5-15 min

This game is hands down my favorite icebreaker to play after breaks (or anytime).

Instructions for Playing

One person starts by saying "I'm a tree!" They stand in the middle and take the shape of a tree.

Two more people stand up and add to the scene as they like. For instance, someone could say "I'm an apple" and they stand up and take the shape of an apple under the tree. Or another might say "I'm a squirrel" and pretend to climb the tree.

Then, the person who was the tree gets to decide who stays: the apple, or the squirrel? "The squirrel stays."

Then it repeats, with the person again saying "I'm a squirrel." And, two new people add to the scene. Maybe one says "I'm a nut" and another says "I'm a cat."
"The cat stays."
"I'm a cat." "I'm cat food." "I'm a crazy cat lady."
"The cat lady stays" etc....
The fun starts when people really think outside the box: "I'm the tree's sense of self-doubt" or, "I'm the squirrel's sexual energy" etc.

Attributions

Daniel Johnson of Authentic Relating Philadelphia.

"How's Yours?"

Setup
Full Group or
Breakout Groups

Time
5-20 min

There are limitless opportunities for creativity in this game.

Instructions for Playing

One person leaves the room. Meanwhile, everyone else decides on a thing which is common to all of them. It could be something simple like a toothbrush, or a bed. Or, it could be something more abstract, like childhood memories, or worries.

After choosing the common thing, the person then re-enters the room and plays a guessing game to discover what was chosen. The only question they ask is "How's yours?" They can ask anybody in the group, and they can ask in any order. Whoever is responding to the question answers with a vague statement describing their thing. It continues until the person is able to guess what the thing is.

Then, that person chooses someone new to leave the room, and the game repeats with a new thing chosen.

Example: The group chooses "toothbrush."
Q: "How's yours?"
A: "Green"
Q: "How's yours?"
B: "Dirty"
Q: "uhhh.... is it dirty laundry?"
Group: "no... keep guessing."
Q: "How's yours?
C: "Used"
etc. etc...

Or, another example, with the thing being childhood memories
Q: "How's yours?"
Answers: "traumatic, beautiful, forgotten, tense, simple..." etc.

Facilitator Instructions

This is an easy game to explain and then get to participate in yourself.

Attributions

Daniel Johnson of Authentic Relating Philadelphia.

Fortune Cookie

This is a great ending game for any event.

Instructions for Playing

Go around the circle. Each person says a word to co-create a sentence or paragraph. When done, this is your fortune cookie message! Repeat it again, with each person saying their same word.

You may acknowledge the brilliance of this fortune by inviting the group to put their hands together, bow, and say "Yes yes yes yes yes" when the repeat is complete.

Facilitator Instructions

Sparkle ninja monkeys nom badass bananas. (You're welcome)

**Whatcha Doin'?

This can be played in a group circle or in pairs. It's a great way to get people loosened up.

Instructions for Playing

One person begins miming an activity. The person next to (or across from) them says, "Whatcha Doin'?" The first person answers with something entirely different from what they are actually doing (for example, if they are pretending to swing a baseball bat, they might say "I'm brushing my teeth").

Then the asker begins miming the activity given in words. The next person in line asks "Whatcha Doin'?" and gets a different answer, etc. Try to answer as quickly as possible, without thinking about it!

Facilitator Instructions

Demo and then play!

Attributions

This is a classic improv game.

Bumblebee

This game is a great mix between improv and authentic relating. It helps participants connect without using content, requires presence in the moment, and is non-threatening enough to use in any social situation.

Introduction: Do you remember the movie "Transformers"? There was the little yellow cab, Bumblebee, whose voice box was broken, so he could only communicate by changing the radio. For the next few minutes, we're only going to talk to each other through our radios.

Instructions for Playing

Demo the game, then form pairs of As and Bs. As sing a few lines - about 10 seconds - from a song, whichever one pops to their mind first. Bs sing a few lines of whatever song they think of in response. They cannot pick any song that they thought of while A was singing. Continue back and forth until 3 minutes is up. Give 1 min for shares within the pairs.

Facilitator Instructions

Singing and instant comebacks are an edge for many people, so this is also a rich game to explore social self-consciousness. If you take shares, be sure to ask both about the fun and the uncomfortable experiences people had while playing.

Variations

· Sing-a-long: Make a circle with the full group. Anybody can start a song, and the rest of the group joins in singing, until somebody begins a new tune. Stop when you stop having fun.

· Rock Battle: Get into breakout groups of 4-7 people. Count off the groups. Group 1 starts a song, organically getting on the same page with each other about what they're singing. After a minute, signal group 1 to stop, and point to Group 2, who has to start singing a song off of Group 1's (whatever comes to their mind), and whose members need to get on the same page about what that group song will be, without direct verbal communication. Continue until all groups have gone a few times. Encourage playful competition between the different groups, seeing which can synergize fastest!

Attributions

Developed by Texas facilitator Mike Blas, with variations from
Sara and the Austin Love Juggernaut.

+Conductor

Setup
Full Group

Time
10-25 min

This is a singing game where someone (of any level of musical talent) makes an improvised song using the group like a human loop recorder. Conductor can be deep, silly, transcendent, or even chaotic. Lots of folks in the Miami community call it their favorite game, especially the Healing Conductor variation.

Instructions for Playing

Form a tight seated circle with the group, close enough that all could hold hands. Section the circle into 3 choirs with roughly equal numbers of singers.

The conductor enters the middle of the circle and takes a moment to connect to themselves in group silence. They then sing a melody and gesture to choir 1 to repeat it. This improvised line can include words, gibberish, guttural sounds or even just a single note. The conductor then creates another melody for choir 2. And another for choir 3.

After 1-2 minutes the conductor gestures for singers to end the song. Then ask if a new player wants to be the conductor. The facilitator goes first to demo the game. Then, others volunteer to go until the energy dips or people tire of singing.

Facilitator Instructions

Conductor can be hauntingly beautiful or messy and chaotic. Here are a few ways to keep it tight: have a musical person go first, have each choir do a practice note or word together to sync tempo, ask people to sing softly, pack each choir with a musical person or two, do some vocal warm-ups or group sing-a-longs before diving in, have participants focus more on melodic lines than beatboxing, have everyone clap together to keep tempo.

Variations

- Healing Conductor: Lead the group in a 1-2 minute meditation where folks will identify a difficult memory or conflict in their life. Take them back there. How does it feel in your body? Who was there? What happened?

  Now, they will split this emotionally charged memory into three parts.

  Part 1 is "The Objective Self." What happened with absolutely no story, narrative or interpretation? What would a video camera record verbatim? Ex. She asked me to cancel my flight to visit her.

  Part 2 is "The Reactive Self." What does your hurt inner child have to say about this situation? All story, not objective at all. Ex. Nobody will ever love me.

  Part 3 is "The Higher Self." What does wisdom have to say about this? Ex. I will find love again. Now people have identified the three parts that will become the three choirs. Bonus points if you have people write down one sentence for what each part is saying. Demo first as facilitator. Feel into what you wrote for The Objective Self and sing a line of that to choir 1. Repeat for Choir 2 as The Reactive Self. And Choir 3 as The Higher Self. Then have everyone repeat the line from The Higher Self and bask in that beautiful wisdom. Because music cuts straight into emotion, this game is very powerful at changing our relationship to difficult memories.

Attributions

Developed by Phil Santos of Ecstatic Playground in Miami.
Inspired by Bobby McFerrin's circle singing.

**+Getting Presents

Setup
Triads/Small groups
(3-4 people)

Time
20 min for triads/25
min for quads

The rapid-fire nature of this game can help when participants are feeling stuck or uncreative. It can unlock gratitude in the receivers even when accepting the idea of gifts is tough. It can be fun and silly and connecting.

Instructions for Playing

Choose a receiver - whoever's birthday it was last.

Say to participants: "Your co-conspirators and you are now at a birthday party. Whose birthday? Each of yours in turn! And you have each brought exciting, wonderful gifts for each other. Lots of 'em! The person with the most recent birthday will be the Receiver first. The others will be Givers.

Receiver: your job is to get wonderful gifts. Meet each gift with joy, enthusiasm, and gratitude. It doesn't matter what it is, the invitation here is to welcome everything and assume nothing. Also, go fast: the presents will keep coming, and that is part of the point!

Giver, your job is to give gifts to the receiver, telling them what you're giving them, pretty quickly. They can be thoughtful or thoughtless, exciting or boring, appropriate or inappropriate. You are invited to avoid preplanning your gifts and give what comes up in the moment. Take turns, and offer a new gift as soon as the receiver has expressed appreciation for the last one."

Play for 4 minutes. Then, invite the group to share with each other before switching: What was it like giving and receiving, in 1 sentence?

Attributions

Old Improv Game. Submitted by David Betz-Zall
from Authentic Seattle

Word Association

Setup
Full Group, Breakout Groups, or Pairs

Time
10 min

Instructions for Playing

Go around the circle (or back and forth if in pairs). Each person says a word related to what the last person shared, as quickly as they can - no censoring the thought.

Facilitator Instructions

Encourage people to relax and not think too much.

Variations

· Categories: Give a category for the words to fall into, ex. colors or animals. The person who can't think of something has to propose the next category.

· Noticing: Each person says a word based on something they're noticing or feeling. Go around again sharing a word, but this time, each person says a word that comes up in association to the word of the person before them. Continue until the circle is complete. Try this with emotions, physical sensations, or all-out noticing.

I Love Myself!

Setup
Pairs, Breakout
Groups, Full Group

Time
7-10 min

A cute twist on improv games, this also serves as an approach to self-talk that may be new for some people.

Instructions for Playing

During each person's turn, they must say something that they love about themselves. If they can't think of something right away, they have to throw their hands up and say "I love everything about myself!"

Facilitator Instructions

Take sharebacks on how this is for everyone, and see how everyone's experiences are different or the same.

Attributions

First experienced with Christine Braboy of the Austin Love Juggernaut. Origin unknown.

Check-In Games

Check-In Games

Facilitators may get good at "reading a room", but we're certainly not telepathic. To know how people are doing, we need to ask. But one of the fastest ways to get a roomful of mumbles is to ask, "How's everyone doing tonight?"

These check-in games give easy and clear ways to a) find out participants' feelings in general or about specific topics; and b) help participants land in a space by bringing their voice into the room. They are as good for the start of a meeting, hangout, or date as they are for anytime during an event.

Map of the Territory

- Rose Bud Thorn, P.I.E.S., and B.D.S.V.G Connection give easy category options for how participants can share their experience of their lives, a topic, or feelings right now.

- Sentence Stems and Spectrum can be used for sharing individual experience, and for getting feedback on the group's state, needs, or perspective on a topic. These are two of the most useful and adaptable games in the manual.

- Secret Identity explores the difference between "authentic" and "inauthentic" greetings. It is helpful for showing new groups what Authentic Relating aims for.

When to use Check-In Games:

- At the beginning of an event, to get everyone's voices in the room and have participants relax by getting to share and be heard
- Anytime in a meeting or social hangout, to invite an easy form for deeper connection
- When you're not sure how the group is doing and want to find out

Index

**+Rose, Bud, Thorn

Rose, Bud, Thorn is a simple way to normalize talking about how things are going, so good things can be celebrated and issues addressed without seeming heavy or overwhelming. I use this game as a check-in to start company meetings, community dinners, and parties. It is simple enough for anyone to pick up quickly, yet can go as deep as people want it to.

Other uses for this game:
As a way to give feedback on projects, group dynamics, or participants' feelings in general. As a relationship reflection game by asking for people who know each other to share a Rose, Bud, and Thorn about their connection. Etc...

Instructions for Playing

Each person shares a Rose, Bud, and Thorn.

> Rose: something that has been going really well.
> Bud: something that is new, interesting, or full of possibility.
> Thorn: something that has been difficult or frustrating.

After each person shares, they choose the person to go next. You can either let the shares end organically, or time them for 90 seconds to 3 minutes per person.

Facilitator Instructions

Whoever is leading the exercise decides whether it's from the past day, week, since the last meeting, etc. and whether they should be from people's work or non-work lives.

An option in this game is to add other prompts, such as "Compost" (what's dying that is giving way to new life), "Weed" (something you would like to eradicate from your life), or anything else you or the group wants to invent.

Attributions

I've seen this game played in many groups and communities, both personal and professional. Origin unknown. The write-up was done by Sara Ness and Norian Caporale-Berkowitz of AuthTeams.

+P.I.E.S

Often we'll ask someone "How are you", and receive "fine" or "good" as a response. This exercise has become a favorite among friends and facilitators as a way of checking in that gives more expansive answers.

Instructions for Playing

In pairs or small groups, each person shares a 1-10 rating, and a longer description of how they are doing Physically, Intellectually, Emotionally, and Socially/Spiritually (P.I.E.S.). Spend 30-60 seconds on each category.

Others listen without interrupting until it's their turn to speak.

Facilitator Instructions

Depending on the size and experience level of the group, the facilitator can either time each person's share, or let groups manage time themselves.

Variations

- For a more creative and challenging version, each person uses a metaphor or an image when describing each category, e.g. "Emotionally, I feel like a volcano that's rumbling and just waiting to explode."

Attributions

Submitted by Jessie Reilley from Brisbane Authentics, learned from Franziska Curran (she possibly learned it from someone else) who would use it as a check-in and bonding exercise with engineering student

+B.D.S.V.G Connection

Playing with my partner at night to connect and share about our day, I noticed that having a practice of saying these things brought us closer together. ~Surelys

Instructions for Playing

Share from your day, or week, or from the last time you've seen each other, in this order:
A Brag, a Gratitude, a Desire, a Vulnerability and a Fear.

Brag - If I had cheerleaders in the backdrop, they would have broken out in dance when I was/wasn't/did/said/didn't say this...

Gratitude - I'm grateful for...

Desire - I want, desire, am compelled towards...

Vulnerability - What wants to be said now/what I would tell my best friend right now/what I'm scared to say...

Fear - Noticing my vulnerability/I noticed I'm scared...

Attributions

Surelys Galano, part of the Boulder CO and Los Angeles groups

**Sentence Stems

Setup
Full Group

Time
10-30 min

Simply put, a "sentence stem" is the beginning of a sentence, for which the rest can be uniquely completed by each person in a pair or group. They are highly effective at building connection between people who are unfamiliar with each other, and just as valuable for close friends seeking deeper intimacy. In fact, they are so commonly used in Authentic Relating that they form the backbone of many other games.

Some Options

· If you really knew me, you would know...
· Something I really appreciate about you [pick a person or go around naming everyone] is...
· My friends / parents / therapist / pet / computer would describe me as...
· I'm really passionate about...
· Something I really love about myself is...
· I'm really f***ing good at...
· Something you'd be surprised to know about me is...
· With you, I feel...
· A perfect day for me would be...
· What scares me most is...

Facilitator Instructions

See the Resources section at authrev.org for a list of Interesting Questions that can be turned into Sentence Stems.

Variations

· Gauntlet: Form two lines, and have sentence stems for each side to answer for 1 minute each answering the stem until time is up.

· Social Stems: One person chooses a sentence for the others in the group to complete, and finishes their own stem last. Then the person to their left chooses a stem, etc. until everyone in the circle has offered one. This is a great game to make social gatherings more honest and inclusive!

**Spectrum

Setup
4-7 People

Time
10-20 min

This is the exercise I use most frequently in all different contexts and groups, because it provides a spectacular opportunity to turn qualitative into quantitative data. Differences become a point of discussion rather than a point of contention.

I've used Spectrum to assess preferred interaction styles in corporate teams ('I like direct feedback given in the moment - I like feedback given over email or in other ways that I have time to process'), to process feelings about environmental change at an EPA workshop ('I feel despair about the environment - I feel hope'; 'I feel like I do a lot to help the environment - I feel like I do nothing to help'), and at more Authentic Relating workshops than I can count. ~Sara Ness

Instructions for Playing

Participants will arrange themselves on a spectrum based on their honest, in-the-moment or identity response to a prompt (see Facilitator Instructions). One end of the room is usually "most" and one is "least". For example, a prompt might be "I'm getting something out of this event", and participants would move to "yes" or "no" sides or anywhere in between. If someone doesn't want to respond to that prompt, they can sit out.

> *Example prompts:*
> **Demographic** (most to least income, attractiveness, age, minority identity)
> **State of Being** (feeling most to least comfortable, belonging, engaged)
> **Values** (caring/not caring about politics, impact, conflict)
> **Self Identity** (yes/no considering self lonely, intelligent, privileged)
> **Group Identity** (most/least powerful, respected, in/out, contribution level)

Facilitator Instructions

In a full group, the facilitator gives a prompt which has a range of possible responses. Facilitators may choose to designate alternative poles other than "most" to "least". Once everyone who wants to play is sorted, take shares, which are often the most insightful part of this game.

Variations

- Spectrum Circle: Instead of arranging on a line, participants place themselves around a circle. Use a chair or other obvious article to denote the ends of the spectrum ("to the left of the chair is most, to the right is least"). This will allow everyone to see each other more clearly than is possible in a line.

- Perception Placement: Once everyone has placed themselves on the spectrum and the facilitator has taken some shares, participants can move others based on their perception of that person. For instance, a prompt of "highest/lowest status in the room" might allow for participants to move others up or down based on how they perceive others' status. If worried about sensitivity, you may want to create a rule of only moving people up on the spectrum, not down.

- Thumb Poll: If leading this exercise online or with groups that don't have freedom of movement, the facilitator can prompt a thumb poll (thumb up = most, thumb down = least, middle = neutral) or a 1-5 or 1-10 finger ranking.

Attributions

This game seems to be used in many different places.
Its origin is unknown.

**Secret Identity

Setup
Full Group

Time
20 minutes

This game stemmed from a desire to explore social norms, and how we choose how deep to be with one another. What is the effect if we aim to keep conversation shallow? What happens if we show ourselves to others but aren't met as we hoped or expected?

This is a fantastic game for showing the difference between Authentic Relating and "default world/normal" connection.

Instructions for Playing

To begin, split the room into two secret groups or identities. One way to pick secret identities is to ask everyone to think about their birthdate (e.g. March 4th). If the day (4th) is even, the participant will start in the Friendly group. If the day is odd, they start in the Raw group. Participants will mill about the room, engaging in quick exchanges of pleasantries.

The Friendly group will focus their interactions on simple answers or shallow interactions.
>   **Partner**: "How are you?", "What's up?", or "How's it going?"
>   **Friendly group**: "Not much, you?" or "Good, you?"

The Raw group may respond with one sentence about something genuinely 'up' in their life. Such as:

>   **Raw group**: "I'm struggling to find meaning in my work. You?" or "I've never felt more satisfied in relationship than I do these days. You?" or "I'm traveling so much that this place doesn't feel like home. You?"

Participants don't know if they will be introducing their Raw self to a Friendly, or vice versa, in any configuration. Spend 4 minutes in the original roles, then switch and mill about the room once more. Lastly, allow 4 minutes for participants to choose their role based on their partner. Allow time for sharebacks on the experience.

Notes

This game was invented by Scott McClellan of Austin Love Juggernaut.

Group
Bonding
Games

Group Bonding Games

It doesn't matter what type of event you're leading. From professional conference to sex party, one thing remains constant: people want to connect. They will often rate the whole event based on the amount and quality of connection they received.

These games give an experience of "shared reality": the understanding that others are living lives similar to yours, and that you are not alone even in experiences you believe are particular or isolating. They are deeply bonding and good for many contexts.

Map of the Territory

· Anybody Else, Walk With Me, and Constellations of Concern reveal truths that seem individual, but often are shared by many people in the room. They promote empathy, and can also be used as a way to gather shares after an experience.

· Group Giving Game and Next... allow group members to name and possibly even meet their needs together.

· One Time... and Freeze Frame are simple storytelling games that are great for old friends, family, and people who are beginners to connection work.

· T-Group is a well-researched way to explore and play out group dynamics.

When to use Group Bonding Games:

· At any time to gather experiences or feelings around a topic, or promote one-to-many connection among all group members

· With new or established groups or communities, to catalyze conversation about similarities, differences, and group dynamics

· At the end of an event, to draw out experiences participants have had

Index

· *Anybody Else
· *Next
· Walk With Me
· *One Time

· Constellations of Concern
· Freeze Frame
· Group Giving Game ("Would Y'all?")
· *T-Group

**Anybody Else

Setup
Full Group

Time
10-20 min

This game can be very playful or very deep, depending on how you context the game and what examples you give.

Instructions for Playing

Set chairs in a circle, with one less chair than the number of people present. The displaced person stands in the center and says something that is true for them - for example, "I'm left handed," "I feel uncomfortable about my height," "I'm attracted to at least one person in this room" - and then asks, "anybody else?"

Anybody who has had the same experience, attribute, etc. stands up and rushes across the circle to a new chair. Participants cannot sit back in the chair from which they stood up, or in the chair on either side of that one.

Play for 10-20 minutes, or until the energy starts to flag.

Facilitator Instructions

Set the context for the game according to how deep or playful you want it to go by doing a demonstration. Remind participants to lean into their edge while also honoring themselves.

Variations

· Go!: After the person in the middle says "Anybody Else," everybody who has had that experience stands up, but does not move until the middle person says, "Go!" This gives participants a chance to see and feel connected with the other people who share that experience, which is especially good when exploring more vulnerable topics.

- I Feel You, Bro: After the person in the middle says "Anybody Else," everybody who has had that experience stands up, looks around, and sits back down. The next person to share self-selects. If the group is already standing, members who feel the "Anybody Else" take a step forward, look around, and step back.

- Optionally, the person who gives the original share can offer a deeper cut, for example: "I feel out of place being here…" people step forwards…. "And I imagine some of you are judging me for my gender identity…" anyone for whom that is also true takes another step forwards; those for whom it becomes true can stand up or step forwards.

- Stembody Else: The facilitator offers a stem for anybody to complete, popcorn-style or going around the circle. Anyone who feels the completion is true in his/her own experience stands up. Participants take a moment to look around the room and see who else is standing, and then all sit down. Another participant completes the stem. After a few completions, the facilitator can offer a different stem. Sharebacks.

- Nobody Else: Try to share something which you don't think will be true for anybody else (with the rule that you can't share a long story particular to your life). If anybody does stand up, they get to decide on some sort of action for the person in the middle to perform! If nobody stands up, the person in the middle gets to pick who goes next.

Attributions

Authentic World, with variations by the Austin Love Juggernaut.

Walk With Me

Setup
Full Group

Time
10-20 min

This game is a great complement to Anybody Else, and the movement tends to get people in a flow of sharing honestly.

Instructions for Playing

One person stands up and begins walking around the center of the group, who are standing or sitting in chairs. As they walk, they say, "Walk with me if..." and share something true about themselves.

Anyone else who shares that experience or attribute gets up and begins walking together around the inside of the circle.

Then, one of the people walking can share "Walk with me if..." and say something else. Those who don't share that sit down, those who do either keep walking or stand up and walk.

Facilitator Instructions

It helps for the facilitator to demo this first.

Attributions

I learned this game from Ruthie Odom of Authentic Relating Boston.

Constellations
of Concern

Setup
Full Group

Time
20-30 minutes

This game is meant to reveal unspoken contexts and demographics that may have participants feeling like outsiders in a group, such that they don't feel safe to fully engage.

Themes of gender orientation, inequality, and other diversity considerations have started to become more prominent in events, and this game looks for a way to address them that doesn't "other" any group (for example, if instead you were to say "let's hear from the women because the men have been talking a lot," this might make the men feel like their voices aren't welcomed).

Instructions for Playing

One person names a context they are aware of in the room, for example, "age disparity" or "different political orientations" or "the fact that we're all able to afford this event". These can also be more personal reveals, such as "I'm aware of my age" or "I'm aware of how much money I make relative to others here."

Others move closer to or further away from the original speaker to the extent that they are aware of that context in a way that affects their experience (you could say "to the extent you've noticed that context" or "to the extent that this is on your mind as well"). Then the speaker can ask for shares from a couple of people. When the topic feels complete, someone else can offer a context and start a new constellation.

Facilitator Instructions

Have an idea of a few contexts that you might name.
You may get questions about what qualifies a context. I define a context as a truth we all share in, that affects all of us whether or not it's spoken. (But if you have a better definition feel free to give that-- context is complicated.)

Attributions

Sara Ness created this game at an Authentic Leadership Training which happened to have 23 women participants and one man. She says: "I didn't just want to call out, "Hey, there's only one man in the group!" - but, I was aware that everyone was aware of the disparity and not speaking it. Constellations of Concern allowed for that context to be spoken and discussed ("I'm aware of the gender disparity in the room") with a greater awareness of how sub-grouping affects our identities in a group, and therefore our sense of belonging."

Group Giving Game
(Would Y'all?)

Setup
Full Group

Time
5-20 min

This game is a variant on the "Giving Game" explained in the Self-Expression Games section. It can be played at any time during the night, but it works really well as an ending game to allow a group that has connected with each other throughout the night to solidify and appreciate that connection. Be prepared for group hugs, cuddle puddles, and a LOT of spontaneous creativity.

Instructions for Playing

Any participant can make a request for the group as a whole to enact. If one person is not comfortable with the request, that person can raise their hand and specify what they would like to change about that activity, either for themselves or for the group. Anyone can stop or change the activity at any time.

Facilitator Instructions

If you have a larger group, consider introducing the "welcoming" hand signal from T-groups (an extended open palm), which can be given by anyone to anyone, and helps encourage requests from members who might be more reticent to speak.

Variations

- Sub-Group Giving Game: Identify sub-groups or demographics. Divide the group by these (ex. women and men, under and over 30, members of different geographical communities, cat lovers and dog lovers, etc.). Each group takes turns deciding on a request and making it of the other group.

- Would You (Go Next?): One person makes a request that focuses on another person, who must then choose the next activity; or a request that focuses on the group, but the asker still chooses who requests next.

Attributions

Invented in Austin

**Next . . .

This is hands down, one of my favorite games - guaranteed to bring forth empathetic connection, and able to become both sweet and intense as participants get shared reality around common desires and needs. ~Sara

Instructions for Playing

Go one by one around the circle. Each person tells the one to their left something that they themself would like to hear. For example: "You're not going to fall apart," "Your mother loves you," "You don't have to be perfect," "You're a wizard, Harry!" It doesn't need to be something they want to hear from that particular person. Complete the circle once, or go around multiple times.

Facilitator Instructions

Clarify that you are speaking to this person directly, as if they were you.

Variations

- Moving: Everyone begins meandering around the room. Each person finds themself in front of somebody. Each person exchanges what they'd like to hear (variation: what they would like to hear from that person!). Find somebody new. After a few rounds, let the group start to self-organize on timing, as in the Handshake Game.

- If Only I Could Tell You...: Each person tells the person next to them something the speaker wishes they could tell somebody else in their life. They can identify the intended recipient or not, as desired.

- Prism: One person says the thing they desire to hear into the group as a whole. Anybody in the group can turn to the person on their left or right, or even across the room, and share that thing (while feeling it). Then, everybody says it back to the person who originally shared.

- Extended Dance Remix: In pairs, A shares something they want to hear. B spends a few minutes asking questions (à la Curiosity), clarifying why this is important to A. B reflects back what A wanted to hear, adding and expanding based on the questions they asked. Finally, A shares what it was like to hear the thing they asked for.

Attributions

The Austin Love Juggernaut made this game up during a round of "Would Y'all". Extended Dance Remix variation comes from Jesse Reilly of Brisbane Authentics.

**"One time..."

Setup
Breakout Groups

Time
5-20 min

This is a fun story telling game with variable depth that can be affected by the context given by the facilitator. I like to play it at bars or social settings especially, and it seems to share the conversation bandwidth more evenly amongst the group. I like to play this game as a warm-up for small groups and it leads into a lot of themes well. ~Mike Blas

Instructions for Playing

This is a storytelling game where we tell one-sentence-long TRUE stories that start with, 'One time...' These one sentence stories can have a comma or perhaps a semicolon but should be quick and in synopsis form in order to keep the shares "hot". Example: "One time I accidentally shot my dog in the leg with a bb gun."

In groups of 2 to 8 players (4 is ideal), one person raises their hand and volunteers to be the leader. After the first share, the person to the left (poker style) tells a story and so on, around through the group.

Facilitator Instructions

Encourage participants not to tell any story they thought of while the person prior was speaking, but instead, to be present to the speaker and wait until that person has finished to notice what story comes to their mind.

You can time the game for any length: some groups can stand 5 minutes while at times I've played at coffee shops or bars for over an hour.

You can also request participants to share stories around a particular theme, ex. "Desire", "Fear", "Stories I don't tell my family", etc.

Variations

- One Time I Noticed...: Take a breath or two after sharing your story and play the "Noticing Game" on how you feel after sharing. For example, "One time I had a threesome." Breath or two. "Remembering that now I feel...happy!"

Attributions

Mike Blas of the Texas Authentic communities formalized this game. He credits its true inception to Chip Hankey, a hypnotist in Berkeley, who played it as an informal game with one of his mentors.

Freeze Frame

Setup
Breakout Groups

Time
15-45 min

Jessica Sagar created this for her dad's birthday dinner. She says: "It was a really fun and playful way to allow my dad to receive attention and appreciation (and he loved it), without it feeling too intense for him. Some actions chosen were more silly, while others reflected something sweet- but all made for fun commentary / observations / acknowledgements of him. And, the game was easy enough to play at a table at a restaurant over the course of a few minutes."

Instructions for Playing

Divide into groups of 4-8 people who all know each other. Have the group pick one person to receive.

Direct everyone (but that person) to close their eyes and pick a quality / characteristic / activity that they associate with the receiver. Then, instruct them to decide on an action or a pose which demonstrates it.

Everyone opens their eyes, and on the count of 3, does their action/pose at the same time and then holds it. Go around the group and have each person share the story about what each pose represents.

Switch to the next receiver, or use this as a birthday-style game for only one person to receive attention for the full time.

Facilitator Instructions

This game should be played with participants who are familiar with each other.

Attributions

Invented by Jessica Sager of the Austin Love Juggernaut.

**T-Group

Setup
Breakout Groups
(4-8 people)

Time
1 hour

T-groups can be an incredible way to explore the we-space, especially with trained facilitators to introduce the practice and a dedicated group to play with.

Instructions for Playing

Use 4 hand signals
1. Agreement (wiggle fingers)
2. Bring it to Now (hold palm up, draw hand down and bring fingers together)
3. Reveal Yourself (open palm facing towards the person you're addressing)
4. Headline (draw a headline in the air)

Break out into groups of 4-8 people, each ideally with someone experienced in T-group, and have an in-the-moment conversation for 40 minutes.

To give context for something you're saying, or mention past or future, say it as a headline. If somebody is giving too much context, use the "Bring it to Now" signal. If someone is asking questions or saying things without revealing their motivations, you can use the "Reveal Yourself" signal (and they can choose whether or not to do so). You can also co-create nonverbal interactions.

At the end of the time, each person gets to do a one-minute "check out".

Attributions

This "game" is a core team-building practice also called "Sensitivity Training Group" that has been around since the 1960s and has been extensively studied by psychologists and sociologists, most noticeably at NTL Laboratories. Google it for more information and to find local groups.

Self Awareness Games

Self Awareness Games

Who are you? Really? Do you know the interaction between your different parts, your values, your shadow and self?

These games are designed to help you and your participants dig into the deeper authentic truth behind who you believe yourself to be.

Map of the Territory

· Core Exploration, Distillation, Story→Headline, and Into the Magic Shop clarify and synthesize what matters to us.

· Split Brain, Emotion Sculpture, and Distinguish Your Shadow explore contradictions between different parts of the self.

· What I Mean By That Is... and Context Conversation let us, and others, see what is beneath the words we use.

· Meet My Essence, Be Your Own Angel, and Who Are You? let us explore our concept of self by introducing ourselves to others in creative ways.

When to use Self Awareness Games:

· To create reliable and powerful depth and consideration, at any time during an event

· When participants seem to have entrenched views about who they are, and you want to shake that up

Index

Core Exploration

This is meant to both help participants get clear on their deepest motivations, as well as to train the skills of empathic listening, curiosity, and reflection.

Instructions for Playing

In triads pick an A, B, and C. A is the Explorer, B is the Listener, C is the Speaker.

A asks C, the Speaker, what matters most to them or why they are here, then spends 3 minutes exploring C's reality.

Tools A might use are:
- Feeling (what you felt when they said the thing, and sharing where you felt them the most)
- Reflecting (reflecting what was said as accurately as possible)
- Digging (asking "Why does x matter to you?" "What else is there about x that feels important to say?")
- Distilling (summarizing what was said and checking to see if the summary lands).

After time is called, B, the Listener, shares "When I felt you the most was..." for 1 minute.

Then, give 2 minutes for A and B to share what they understand now about what matters most to C.

Allow 1 minute for C to share what they understand now about what matters most to them. (Optional: Give a few minutes for C to journal on what they took away.)

After each person has gotten a chance to go, come back to the whole group, and each person shares one sentence to the group that encapsulates the core of what matters most to them.

Facilitator Instructions

You can play with using different prompts to help explore other topics, and/or adding or subtracting tools that encourage getting somebody else's world.

Attributions

Developed by Sara Ness for the Authentic Leadership Training.

Distillation

A variant on the Empathy Game, this is designed to help participants get to the heart of what is most important to them about a topic.

Instructions for Playing

In groups of 3, designate an A, B, and C.

· As have 2 minutes to speak to something on their heart (or other prompt, ex. "Why I'm here" or "What matters the most to me").
· B's reflect, for 45 seconds, exactly what they heard.
· A's have 1 minute to clarify, add context, or reiterate.
· C's share what they got out of the whole process for 45 seconds.
· A's sum up the heart of their share in one sentence.
· Come back to the whole group and each person shares their sentence.

Variations

· Mix it Up: A's share for 2 minutes. B's reflect for 1 min, C's reflect for 1 min. A's clarify, add context, or reiterate for 1 minute. B's share what they got from the whole process for 30 seconds, C's share what they got for 30 seconds. A's sum up the heart of their share in one sentence. Group shares.

Attributions

Developed by Isaac Cohen of the Austin Love Juggernaut.

+Story → Headline

Setup
Pairs

Time
15 min

This is a great game for inviting people to get out of the details of a story and into what's most alive about it for them. People sometimes find that the point of their story isn't what they had thought it was! It's also a great game for very verbal people to try a "shorter can be sweeter" style of storytelling.

Instructions for Playing

One person is the Storyteller or SHARER and tells the same story THREE TIMES. Each time the story should get shorter and more to the point. The LISTENER pays attention and then briefly shares impact at the end.

SHARERS share the story 3 times:
FIRST ~ 1 minute
SECOND ~30 seconds
THIRD ~10 seconds
30 sec - LISTENER shares impact
Switch
Partner Share (2 minutes)
Whole Group Share (3 min)

Facilitator Instructions

Ask the SHARERS to think about ONE THING that is alive for them.
Examples:
· What is most scary right now
· Something you love
· Anything else that's alive for you!

To get the most out of this game, repeat the same story 3 times rather than continuing it.

Attributions

Who knows? Submitted by David Betz-Zall of Authentic Seattle

**Meet My Essence

This game was designed for a Games Night whose theme was "Shadow Side," as a way to ease people back into deeper exploration after the break. "This turned out to be a super powerful, intimate way to get to know people. I thought it would be light, but turned out to be quite the easy way into a deep dive, and most people's favorite game of the evening. It became tender, with plenty of space for risk & honesty with communication seeming straightforward (vs. an intense or soft-and-gooey moment)." ~Erin Brandt

Instructions for Playing

Everyone stands up and walks around, shaking hands with and introducing themselves to people around the room. Introduce yourself as your Initial Self, the self you FIRST show to people. Speak the HOW and WHY you are showing up that way. Person being met simply says "Hi! Welcome." Examples:

"Hi! I'm Erin! When I first meet people, I am super cheerful because I actually feel warm and cheerful and a rush to lean in and eagerness and curiosity to meet new people. Not being welcomed and included is super painful to me, so I make sure I welcome and include others, especially if they are new."

"Hi, I'm John. I'm really loving and warm and soft when I meet people, so you HAVE to love me. It would be devastating to me if you found something to be displeased with, or not love me right from the beginning.

Play until everyone who wants to, gets to introduce themselves. For a small group, all stay seated or standing in a circle, and one person approaches another across the circle and greets them while everyone else listens.

Variations

Meet my Light and Shadow: Close your eyes, and get in touch with the self that emerges when you feel under-resourced. This might be the self you repress, fear, or judge. Then open your eyes, and say you'll be introducing yourself as that self, and WHY you show up like that. You can use the sentence stem: "Hi, I'm___I'm going to___because__" For example:

> "Hi, I'm Sara! I'm going to be SUPER loud and energetic, because if I put off enough energy, you're sure to like me and then I don't have to be as anxious about what you're experiencing or what you think of me."

> "Hi, I'm Sara. I'm going to be really, really concerned about your experience, so that you feel seen and validated and included and I get to make up for all the times in my childhood that I didn't feel that way."

Then close your eyes again and now get in touch with your light side - the self you become when you're feeling at your best. Repeat the whole process with light side. Then give shares.

Facilitator Instructions

Ask for volunteers to demo in front of the group. After a few demos, let people know that they can introduce multiple sides, and then give them 5-10 minutes to mill around and make introductions. Then, have people sit down again. Take some shares.

Attributions

Erin Brandt, a long-time Authentic World/AMP coach and founder of the "Appreciating Men" workshops, with variation by Sara Ness.

**Who Are You?

Setup
Pairs

Time
15 min

This is one of the more powerful identity-challengers I've found. It quickly gets to the heart of the questions we ask ourselves and others about
who we are.

Instructions for Playing

Pair up and choose an A and a B.
A will be asking B questions to start with. The first question A asks B is:
"Who are you?"

B has 2 minutes to respond. Then, A asks:
"Who do you pretend to be?"

B responds for 2 minutes. Then, this time, B asks A:
"Who do you think I am?"

A responds for 2 minutes. Take a minute or two to debrief. Then switch roles.

Facilitator Instructions

It can be helpful to have the questions written out somewhere for all to see, or written on note cards.

Attributions

From Patrick Wolf of Authentic L.A.

**Split Brain

Setup
Triads

Time
30-45 min

This game uses core concepts from Internal Family Systems therapy to externalize an internal discussion. Generally, the game is clarifying and fascinating for all involved!

Instructions for Playing

In groups of three, decide who will speak first.
Do a connect-to-self meditation, during which the speaker focuses on discovering two parts of themselves that seem at odds.

When the meditation completes, the speaker names the parts and describes the way these two parts speak to them. Then they assign one part to each of the other two people.

For 5 minutes, the two people representing the different "parts" will have a conversation while the speaker acts as the director, feeding each lines or adjustments to make the conversation more accurate to what is happening inside the speaker's own head.

Take a minute to debrief as a group, then switch to another member's voices.
Optionally, the game can be played in pairs, where the speaker takes on one of their own roles.

Variations

Dissonance Doctor: Choose a speaker and a listener for each part of the dissonance. The speaker has 3 minutes to share a dissonance between two sides of themselves, while each listener's role is to key into the particular part of the dissonance that they were chosen for.

Each listener then has 1 minute to reflect back the side of the dissonance they were tracking. No assessments, just reflection.

The speaker has 1 more minute to add/clarify anything else that came up for them from the listener's share.

Each listener then has 2 minutes to share the impact of their listening to their side of the dissonance: What do they get about that part?

Attributions

This game seems to have been in the field, as it was invented simultaneously by Sara Ness and Jessica Tartaro in the same week, and probably lots of people before that. Dissonance Doctor was created by Chad Phillips of the Austin Love Juggernaut.

**Context Conversation

Setup
Pairs

Time
10-20 min

Context Conversation has become Sara's favorite way to inspire self-awareness, and helps participants get at a key point of authentic relating: understanding their own motivations, and others', for how they choose to act in any moment. She has played this for hours with partners, and likes to drop it into casual conversation. The game also could be played in a group of 3-5 people. There are almost infinite levels of context for anything we express, so there's never an end to the game!

Instructions for Playing

In pairs, say hello for a minute, then have a context conversation. Go back and forth using the sentence stem "Right now, I would...because..." "Right now" speaks to the behavior you would do, and "because" is the motivation. What is the intent behind that expression? Why do you want to say it, here, now, to this person?

For instance:
"Right now, I would write clear instructions for this game, but go back and edit each sentence multiple times... because I want to look good for all of you, so that you'll respect me and think I know what I'm talking about." Or, "Right now, I would ask you a question, because I feel nervous and don't want the attention on me."

The "because" is a deeper reveal of feeling, belief, or motivation, and could go multiple levels down ("I would, because....because...." etc).

Facilitator Instructions

To pair up my favorite way of doing this is to go around and have each person say "Oh" or "Yeah" by turns. Oh's turn to their right, Yeah's to the left - insta-pairs!

Tell participants to be aware of both the thoughts and beliefs that are motivating them, and the bodily sensations and emotions that affect the interaction.

It can be hard to know whether to respond to the behavior or the because. Let participants know that they can say their "right now...because..." in response to either, and if they get stuck, come back to what's happening in the moment.

Variations

Building Up To It: Context Conversation is a complex game, so here are some ways you can make it easier to introduce:

Add the "because" later in the game: Start with just saying "Right now, I would..." "Hearing that, I would...." back and forth with your partner.
Use the sentence stem "I want to...": For example, "I want to give a good example here, because seeming intelligent is a big part of my identity." This is easier for some people than "Right now, I would..."

Attempted Normalcy: Either begin with normal conversation and switch into Context Conversation, or switch into normal conversation after playing a round of Context. Debrief in the pairs about how this is different.

Attributions

Developed by Sara Ness, inspired by the best OkCupid message I ever received.
It started something like, "Casual greeting. Compliment on an aspect of your profile! Affirmation of similar interests...." Yes, I went on a date with him.

**Emotion Sculpture

Setup
Pairs

Time
10-20 min

This game can be an opportunity to explore an emotion you struggle with and would like to address. The intention should not be to fix or heal these emotions, but simply see and address it sincerely, in whatever manner arises.

Instructions for Playing

In pairs, person A will be the Sculptor and B the Sculpture, such as made with modeling clay or a wooden carved figure. A takes about a minute of silent meditation to choose an emotion for the other person to embody. It can be any (loud) emotion.

A describes to the model how that emotion feels in their body and what they imagine it looks like. B begins to position themselves accordingly. As the emotion is being embodied, A can request minor tweaks, like the director of a scene. Ex: "Shoulders more hunched, brows more furrowed. I think it would be standing more upright," etc.

Once A feels satisfied with the physical manifestation of their emotion, they move completely around their "sculpture" to take it in as much as possible. Then, A can begin to verbally address that emotion with sincerity. This could involve giving it compassion to let it soften, yelling at it, crying, etc. After they address the emotion, B can return to a neutral state. Switch roles and allow another moment of meditation for each to settle into their new role and B to pick an emotion.

Sharebacks can occur in pairs or full group (or both).

Facilitator Instructions

Give a full, if slightly shortened, demo of every step. This is very important to set the tone. Encourage both A and B to be connected to their sensations during the process.

Variations

· Embodied Emotion: In pairs, one person is the "Living Statue" and one is the "Witness." The facilitator (or witness) names an emotion and the "Living Statue" embodies their experience of the personification of that word for 15-30 seconds. The "witnesses" take in their chosen embodiment, noticing what imaginings, judgments, or comparisons arise. Take 1-2 minutes for each to share impacts of what it was like to embody and what it was like to witness.

Attributions

Created by Indigo Townsend.

Distinguish Your Shadow

Instructions for Playing

In groups of 4-7, each person has 10 minutes to introduce their shadow / alter ego / a part of themselves that they hide or are ashamed of. The other members of the group can ask the shadow questions, such as
· "How do you most like to be seen?"
· "What do other people need to be for you to show up that way?"
· "What do you say or do to be seen that way?"
· "What's underneath the desire to be seen that way?"

The person embodying their shadow responds as that part of themselves. They can also walk around and interact as the shadow. At the end, thank that person, and switch.

Variations

Shadow Conversation: Have each person in the group go around and identify their shadow, and its attributes, for 1-2 minutes. Then, for 10 minutes the group holds a conversation or does a group activity as their shadows - for example, "Plan a vacation for all of you", or "Discuss asking somebody to prom". Debrief.

Golden Shadow: Participants introduce and embody their golden shadows - the part of them that they think most serves them, or of which they are most proud, or that most absolutely rocks! Answer questions/hold a conversation as this self.

Attributions

Originally developed by Authentic World, with variations by Sara Ness and Jordan Allen for Integral Austin.

Shadow Criticism

Setup
Pairs or Breakout
Groups

Time
15-30 min

This game can be an opportunity to explore an emotion you struggle with and would like to address. The intentions should not be to fix or heal these emotions, but simply see and address it sincerely, in whatever manner arises.

Instructions for Playing

In pairs or small groups. Designate one person (A) to talk for 1-3 minutes about a criticism that they have of the experience, its presentation, and/or the facilitators. Then the other group member(s) spend 3-5 minutes inquiring about the shadow aspect of that criticism.

For instance, if A is dissatisfied with the lack of edginess in an exercise, shadow elements could be A's desire to push him or herself regardless of what others might be needing, A's propensity for following instructions over demanding value, A's desire for the current moment to be different, etc. Sharebacks (or group sharebacks) and switch.

Facilitator Instructions

Emphasize that the game is not intended to invalidate members' opinions, but to help them explore their internal processes even during the survey stages of a transformational experience.

Attributions

From Integral facilitator Diane Hamilton.

Be Your
Own Angel

Setup
Full Group

Time
15-20 minutes

Instructions for Playing

Group stands in a circle with a chair-back, pillow, etc. in front of them as a symbolic barrier.

Everyone closes their eyes while one person leads through a meditation (see facilitator instructions). During the meditation, each person searches for an aspect or way of being they'd like to step into. If it feels good or right, they voice out loud what they want to step out of, then physically step over the barrier as they name what they are stepping into.

Once inside the circle, each person greets others as the version of themselves they're stepping into. Then everyone mingles, introducing themselves as that version of themselves as they step into the circle.

Facilitator Instructions

Start the meditation by guiding them to find something within themselves that they would like to leave behind, let go of, step out of, reminding them to still love themselves in that space.

Demo the greeting others as the version of themselves they're stepping into.

When we played this for the first time, half of the developing team played music and sang words inspired by the group as the event unfolded, which added a lot of depth and power to the overall experience and is recommended.

Attributions

Developed by: Kai Koru (Austin) Jonathan Van Matre (Austin), Rob Razmah (Austin) Shane Orton (Austin), Sara Katelyn Yeater/Sky (Houston), and Katie Stellar Dutcher (Austin). This game was a group led gift at the Fall 2017 Authentic Leadership and Facilitation Training.

Into the Magic Shop

Setup
Pairs and Full Group

Time
10-15 minutes

This game was inspired while reading Into The Magic Shop by James R. Doty and Tinker Dabble Doodle Try by Srini Pilla. It brings us into our desired future as if that existed here and now, and thereby makes the dream more real.

Instructions for Playing

Participants get into pairs. Each person has 1-2 minutes to talk about specific life goals and what they want to achieve.

Then, each participant visualizes and meditates on what that would look like in the future, having achieved these things. Try viewing each scene from different angles.

Take 2 minutes to talk about your visualizations and what they felt like.

Then go back into the meditation and add more detail.

Facilitator Instructions

Use these questions to help guide the visualizations:
What do you see when you look at yourself? What is in front of you? What happens next and what does the new scene bring? Let the positive feelings wash over. Include other aspects of your life in this visualization. What might your dating life, social life, or work life, hobbies, or passions look like in relation to these new achievements?

For added detail:
What does the scene look like now? How did you achieve this?

Attributions

Shane Orton of the Austin Love Juggernaut

Self Expression Games

Self-Expresion Games

Context is powerful. In the right container, we can even surprise ourselves with our authentic expression. Who knows what will come out until we're given the deep space to let out our deepest joys, shadows, and everything in between?

Self-expression games create an opportunity for us to dig up the hidden contexts that govern our days, weeks, months and lives. They are powerful tools to plunge the murky truths dormant inside of us and catalyze new Ways Of Being.

Map of the Territory

· Mudra Theatre is a powerful way to bring expression improvisationally.

· Angels in the Closet and What I Mean By That Is...prompt deeper sharing about experiences and meaning.

· Complain Game and Emotional Volume Knob challenge and explore the level or intensity we are comfortable bringing.

· The Yes/No Game, Request Training, and Stop explore our relationship with power and boundaries as well as help us explore our concept of self by introducing yourself to others in creative ways.

When to use Self Awareness Games:

· Towards the middle or end of a session

· When you want to create transformational moments that participants will remember way after the event

· When dealing with themes of boundaries, desire, and greater self understanding

Index

**Mudra Theater

Setup
Full Group

Time
10 min-1 hour

This is an Austin favorite. We love playing this for hours at community hangouts, especially in the evening and/or around a campfire. ~Sara Ness

This game turned out to be super potent and a fun, easy introduction to circling. The participants talked about the stage/space as if it were a roller-coaster ride and a mystical spot where things were radically surreal and edgy. People couldn't wait to be next. The wildest part is that there's no 'right way' to be there... no reference points. Of course, the next pointing-out instruction was to notice how much we structure our lives to avoid the reality that every moment has this degree of mystery, unknowing, and radical freedom. ~ Robert McNaughton

Instructions for Playing

Create a 'stage' by turning all the chairs towards one side of the room. One participant (self-selected) walks to center stage and meets the space. That person can express whatever they want for a period of time, either timed or gauged by the facilitator to let them cook a bit. The only rule is, the center person can't do anything they previously thought about, so any expression arises newly from the present space.

After the expression time is over, the rest of the group can share what they notice, appreciate, are curious about, etc..., basically a few minute-long turbo-circle.

Variations

- Mudra Leader: Have a "leadership stick" in the middle of the room. Form a circle around that. Anybody can step in the middle and become the leader for 6 min, but cannot do anything they thought of before picking up the stick! Leadership can be whatever it means to you. After each person goes, have 3 minutes and/or 2 shares of impact from the group: what did you notice in their leadership? What worked for you? The person then has the option to ask for 1 critical share or 1 positive share if they desire.

Attributions

Developed by Robert MacNaughton, with variation by Sara Ness.
Based on practices Chogyum Trungpa Rinpoche brought to the Boulder community when he began the Naropa Institute.

Angels in the Closet

Setup
Pairs or Breakout Groups

Time
15-45 minutes

This is a cathartic way to reveal some of the deepest parts of our history, good and bad. When playing the variation Angels and Skeletons, an optional Hot Seat can be played after to dive even deeper.

This game works well with a theme as well. I often used it during pandemic-times in 2020, for participants to talk about their Angels (places they felt they showed up in alignment with the person they want to be, personally or interpersonally) and Skeletons (places they fell short of who they try to be) during quarantine.

Instructions for Playing

Each participant has 3-5 minutes to talk about the "angels in my closets"- all the accomplishments and events you're most proud of in your life. Be as open and boastful as you're comfortable being, and even a little more than that. After each share, others in the group can respond with what they appreciated most or were most struck by in the share.

Variations

- Skeletons and Angels: One participant spends 3-7 minutes talking about the skeletons (things they're most ashamed of) in their closets. The format for "One Time" can be used, such as "One time I disappointed myself when..." etc. Then, take about 3 minutes to talk about the angels.

Attributions

From Sara Ness of Authentic Revolution/The Austin Love Juggernaut.

**What I Mean by That Is...

So often, we use words and phrases without shared understanding of what they mean, which leads to pain and confusion down the road. I use this game all the time now in daily life. "I want you to get back to me about this soon. And what I mean by soon is..." etc.

Instructions for Playing

Partner up and choose A and B. A says to B: "I love you. And what I mean by that is..." They then define the phrase based on what it means to them in this connection.

For example, "What I mean by that is the facilitator told me to tell you I love you, so I did." or, "What I mean by that is I enjoy your company and feel close to you."

Then B answers the phrase in their own way: "I love you, and what I mean by that is..." You can also use different phrases, such as "I understand you", "I respect you", "I hate you", etc.

It can help to start soft, with phrases like "I like you" and build up to more intense definitions.

Attributions

Invented by Elisabeth Brustein of Authentic Dallas.

Complain Game

Setup
Pairs

Time
10-15 minutes

The purpose of this game is to get people directly in touch with their inner wisdom. The Tantrum variation helps explore the underlying needs which complaining is attempting to fulfill. One possibility: it allows us to be emotionally expressive, and then acknowledges that our needs aren't about other people.

Instructions for Playing

In pairs, decide on an A and B. First, partner A talks for 2 minutes about a situation in their life that they are not satisfied with - an area where they want something to be different or better. COMPLAIN! Either take a negative view of the situation as if you were in a bad mood, OR really amp it up and talk about this place as a victim. Afterward, partner B does the same thing for 2 minutes.

Then partner A gets into the 'Voice Of Their Higher Self' (or speaks from their most resourceful self or state they are aware of). For 3 minutes, A speaks to B as if that person were A's usual self. Start with the stem: "(A's name), This is Your Higher Self speaking. I heard what you have said, and I want to respond." Partner B does the same thing for 3 minutes. Give shares at the end.

Variations

- +Tantrum!!: Exaggerate your complaining by throwing a tantrum! Be aware of the noise - if you need to go into the lobby or to another space that's ok. Remember to honor yourself while tantruming. Partner witnesses and then, after 3-5 minutes, gives Higher Self advice. Same thing for 3 minutes. Give shares at the end.

Facilitator Instructions

Be open to where people find themselves with this. In the Tantrum variation, people often get really physical. Sometimes things can get silly, sometimes people have had big reactions and want some care afterward. A participant who is a black man talked to us about how powerful the experience was for him, and how he couldn't bring himself to really let go because he had to button down so tightly for work and life that he felt he could never regain his equilibrium if he really tantrummed. It brought home how race can be a big factor (and barrier, but maybe also a portal?) in authenticity.

Attributions

Complain Game developed by Jason Digges of the Integral Center.Tantrum variation developed by David Betz-Zall & Kasia from Authentic Seattle for a game night called "Playing Like a Child."

Emotional Volume Knob

Setup
Pairs

Time
5-15 minutes

This game is about playing within the range of emotional expression. It is a fun way to shift the perspective towards how we are expressing versus the content of our words. It often helps participants be more present in the moment and less worried about "saying the right thing".

Instructions for Playing

In pairs, Person A will be the Conductor, and person B the Expressor. Person A will conduct B in their expression using hand signals as follows:

Fist near hip: Person B stops talking.

Pointing forward: Person B starts talking.

Pointing down: Person B speaks with no emotional expression, dry and rational.

Pointing up: Person B speaks entirely in their emotion expression, losing rationality.

Pointing anywhere between up and down: Person B adjusts to that approximate level.

Take 2 minutes in these roles and then switch.

Facilitator Instructions

Invite conductors to search and play along the expressor's edge.

Attributions

Introduced by Rob Hamshar who brought it from his improv comedy work.
Later applied by Shane Orton towards his Social Freedom Tribe.

**The Yes/ No Game

Setup
Pairs

Time
5-10 minutes

This is hands-down the easiest and fastest way I've found of priming participants' ability to set boundaries and respect themselves. Practicing saying "No" makes us more able to say it later on, and also brings to light how difficult that can be.

This game is also great for noticing our habitual patterns around agreement. Is the "Yes" always a question? Do you have to shut the other person out to say a "No"? Do you want to say "Yes" as soon as the other person gives a "Maybe"? Are you trying to manipulate the other person into a certain response by how you give your own?

Instructions for Playing

In pairs one person is a "Yes" and the other person is a "No". For 1 minute, this is the only word each person can say, going back and forth saying "Yes" and "No" to each other while sticking to their assigned roles.

Notice how it feels to be a "Yes" when someone else is saying "No", or a "No" when they're saying "Yes". Is it okay to hold a boundary, even if the other person presses? Can you say Yes to the other person, even if they are saying no to you?

Switch roles and then give shares.

Variations

· Yes/No/Maybe: For a second round, either person has the option to say yes, no, or maybe as they feel genuinely called to in response to the other person's yes, no, or maybe. Play for 2 minutes and then take shares.

· Desire Calibration: A asks for things that he/she desires from B, and B says "yes", "no", or "maybe" (either according to their genuine desire, or you can mandate one response each round). This can be played with one partner, or mingling and stopping before different partners for multiple rounds. Optionally, play "Would You" afterwards.

Request Training

Setup
Pairs

Time
5-15 minutes

Tools:
Dice, candy, or other small object

This game is good as a precursor to the Giving Game or for a theme on Desire. It helps participants to distinguish when they actually want to say yes or no to a request, what patterns they tend to use in trying to get things they want from somebody else, and how they relate to power dynamics.

Instructions for Playing

In pairs choose who is A and who is B.

B will be asking A for a die (or other small object) for a couple minutes. A can say either no, or give the die if they truly feel that B is authentic (or convincing). B should try to be as authentic in their requests as possible (let their desire and intention be felt without manipulation)

If A gives B the die, B should give it back, and B keeps asking until time runs out, no matter how many times they get the die.

Switch roles and play again. Full-group shares.

Facilitator Instructions

Add some sentence stems for A to answer before the partners switch, for example: "I felt you the most when.." "I gave/didn't give you the die when I felt.." "A pattern I noticed in how you asked was...and the impact was..."

Variations

- Saying No: A must always say no, however B asks.

- Conviction Game: B can use any means possible to convince A to give them the die. Have partners negotiate boundaries first (e.g. "no aggressive physical contact").

Attributions

Invented by Authentic Houston

Stop

This game is great for teaching people to recognize when their power and honest desire is being felt. We often played this game during facilitator trainings.

Instructions for Playing

Participants stand across the room from each other.
Partner A starts walking across the room.
Partner B tries to get A to halt before passing B, using only the word "Stop" (hand gestures can also be allowed, but no physical contact).
A should only stop if he/she truly feels a desire to do so.
A then goes back to the other side of the room and repeats for 3-5 min.
Give pair or group shares, then switch roles and/or partners.

Facilitator Instructions

Stress that the goal is not to manipulate your partner into stopping, but to make them want to do so because they feel and trust your intention.

Attributions

Developed in the early days of Authentic Houston.

Perspective
Shifting
Games

Perspective Shifting Games

Most of us walk around believing that things really are the way we see them. Whether the subject be ourselves, other people, the group field, or intellectual topics about the world, we usually don't question our perspective until we're given a gentle pattern interrupt.

Perspective shifting games give participants space to zoom out and imagine a new reality. They begin questioning the narratives they usually take for granted and change their relationship to them. Powerful stuff.

These games do well when you give a strong narrative for them (why you chose to lead them for this group, in this event).

Map of the Territory

· Change and The Reframe Game allow others to challenge or shift our view of an event or problem.

· Owning Our Judgments, What If..., Trading Faces, and Authentic Goodbye ask us to step into another side of our own perspective.

· Perspective Yoga and The Seems prompt us to explore our perspective from four different angles.

· Try Me On and Congregation of Believers let us see ourselves from the outside in

When to use Perspective Shifting Games:

· Middle to late in your sessions
· When you're working with conflict or change in a group

· When you want to challenge entrenched beliefs, identities, and concepts to open participants up to new teachings or experience

Index

· *Change
· Authentic Goodbye
· The Reframe Game
· Perspective Yoga
· *Owning Our Judgements

· The Seems
· What If...
· Try Me On
· Trading Faces
· Congregation of Believers

**Change!

This game is mainly fun, but it can be quite deep if you pay attention to notice your patterns when you change your story, and how this might reflect how you approach life.

For example, when playing this at the Integral Center, I noticed that my partner, a successful businessman, always changed his story to the direct opposite of what he just said. He recognized that this mirrored how he always approached life at extremes, flipping 180 degrees when dissatisfied with something in daily existence. He went on to sell all his belongings and decided to start taking life as it comes, one day at a time. I didn't point out that this was the exact opposite of what he'd been doing so far.

Instructions for Playing

In pairs, one person in each pair (A) begins telling a story. At any point, their partner (B) can say, "Change!" and A has to change the last thing they said.

Play for 3-5 minutes per partner, then take shares.

Variations

- Truthful: Participants tell a true story from their life

- Therapeutic: Participants tell a true story with emotional charge for them. When B says "Change", A changes to what they would have liked to have happened, or what they would have wanted the situation to be. (This game works almost like Gestalt therapy - very powerful)

- Perspectival: When B says "Change", A changes to another point of view (of somebody else in the story, or a different frame to see the situation through).

- A Little More...: Partner B (saying "change") can instead encourage a little more... something. E.g. "Change...a little more emotion", or "change...more ridiculous!" I like to encourage emotions, but leaving it open also yields fantastic results.

Attributions

I first played this game at the Integral Center in Boulder, although I've found analogs of it in improv work.

94

+The Reframe Game

Setup
3-4 people

Time
20-30 min

We are, collectively, smarter than any of us alone. This game allows for advice to be given on a problem, in a way that is more focused than "what I would do if I were you is..."

Instructions for Playing

In a group one person will talk about a problem they're working with - ideally a difficult conversation, but it could also be a difficult life decision. Give a brief general overview for 2 min, and then ask for a reframe either on the whole problem or a sepcific piece.

When you pause, others in your group can suggest reframes: different ways of looking at or thinking about the problem.

After receiving a reframe, you can either explore a different part of your dilemma, or explore aspects of the reframe. (5 min total per person)

To give everyone a chance to practice, no Reframer can speak twice until everyone has reframed or passed at least once.

Attributions

Invented by Sara Ness and Geof Krum for Authentic Revolution's "Art of Difficult Conversations" class

**Owning Our Judgments

The purpose of this game is to help us see how problems "out there" often reflect an uncomfortable internal experience "in here" that is more vulnerable to admit.

It also helps show the difference between "I feel _____ [emotion word]" and "I feel like _____ [usually a judgment]".

Instructions for Playing

Go around in a circle, and each person shares an unowned value judgment that's true for them in the moment. "I feel like _____" is good for this.
For example, "I feel like this game is stupid."

You're going to not authentically relate for this round and that's okay. Remember your judgment for round two.

In the second round, each person repeats their judgment, and then shares a deeper inner felt experience that the judgment points to or covers over. "When I say 'I feel like _____[judgment],' what's more true for me is that I feel _____ [inner felt experience]."

For example: "When I say 'I feel like this game is stupid,' what's more true for me is that I feel unsatisfied and crave something more edgy."

For round two, if the original judgment is no longer alive, create a new one for the purpose of speaking a deeper truth.

Give shares to debrief and explore the contrast between judgements and felt experience.

Facilitator Instructions

The facilitator should go first in both rounds to give clear examples to work with.

Attributions

Created by Josh Stein of Circling Wizardry.

What if...

Setup
Pairs or Breakout
Groups

Time
15 min

This is a great one for helping people get in touch with their deepest desires, and then ground them into reality. In effect you are playing "The Noticing Game..." on imagined future states.

"What if..." might work particularly well partnered with "Next".

Instructions for Playing

In pairs or small groups, go around the circle, or back and forth, with each person having a chance to share an imagined future state starting with the sentence stem, "What if....?" Example- "What if I loved myself just as I am?"

After that share, imagine how it would feel if that future state were already true. You can share how you feel with the group. After taking enough time to "root into" the feeling you would feel if the state were already true, signal to the next person in the group that it is now their turn.

Variations

· "See Me Now": After a round or two of "What if...?", invite the next participant in line to share their desired future as a statement, ex. "I am in a loving, monogamous relationship" or "I love myself just as I am." Then that person closes their eyes to let that feeling sink in. Once they feel present to the state, they can open their eyes, repeat the phrase, and say, "See me now."

· The group is invited to witness this person as if they had already fulfilled their desire. After a minute, the subject can pass attention to the next person (or, optional, share what that was like). This whole process can happen on participants' own time or be metered by a facilitator.

Attributions

From Mike Blas of the Austin community.

Trading Faces

Setup
Pairs

Time
10-15 Min

"Trading Faces" naturally evolved out of trying to see myself from the outside.

Guy Sengstock and I were talking, and I (Sara) noticed that I felt uncomfortable receiving compliments. I started wondering what I must look like to the world, and created this practice so that I could get either positive or negative feedback from others.

Instructions for Playing

Participants find a partner, introduce themselves, and choose who will be "A" and who is "B". Then both come to silence.

As imagine how they must seem to B's...if they were looking at their own face at the moment, their words and body movements, how would it look from the outside? How would B's feel about them?

As share: "I must seem..." or "I must look..." and describe, for 2-4 minutes, how they think they appear to their partner. Optional, extend for another 2-4 minutes and A's describe how they think they appear to people in general (represented by the person in front of them).

Once the time is up, B's can share feedback for 2-3 minutes, either in an open format or using sentence stems like: "You seem..." "Where I felt you the most was..." and "What I feel with you is..."

Facilitator Instructions

Guide the participants' attention by reading these questions while they are in silence: "If you were looking at your own face at the moment, listening to your words, seeing your body movements, how would it look from the outside? How would B feel about you?" Then, give the "I must seem..." or "I must look..." prompts to start their sentenc

Variations

- Light and Dark: Participants share things they see as positive "seems" for themselves, then negative "seems".

Attributions

Developed unexpectedly by Guy Sengstock and Sara Ness.

Authentic Goodbye

Setup
Pairs, Triads, or
Breakout Groups

Time
15-30 min

This game is based on a good-bye ritual for couples breaking up that is presented in the book Make-Up Don't Break-Up.

The intention of this game is to say goodbye to someone or to some part of yourself. It is helpful to choose a relationship that you are cognitively over but not emotionally over yet. This is especially powerful to do in triads.

Instructions for Playing

Divide participants into pairs, triads, or small groups. Designate an A and a B to go first.

Person A lies on the floor, still and with their eyes closed, as though they were dead. Person B announces what person A is representing to them--i.e. what they are saying good-bye to. Person A remains still and quiet until the end of the experience for Person A. Person A then has 5 minutes to complete the following sentence stems, repeating them as desired during that time:

     One thing about our future that I am saying goodbye to is...
     One thing I will miss about you is...
     One thing I won't miss about you is...
     One thing I wanted to say to you is...
     One way my life is different without you in it is...

Then take time to say goodbye. Consider a gesture to make the goodbye complete. A takes a minute to close eyes and feel their body. When ready, B de-roles Person A by declaring that they are now no longer A's surrogate and are themselves again. Repeat for each partner in the group.

Attributions

Introduced to the AR community by Becky Kangas in Austin, TX.

Perspective Yoga

Setup
Pairs or Breakout Groups

Time
10 min

This game is good for helping people understand the different perspectives that can be taken in a conversation.

Instructions for Playing

Participants have 4 conversations (timed for 2-3 minutes each):

1) With their attention and communication only about themselves,
2) With their attention and communication only about their partner(s),
3) With their attention and communication only about the connection between them,
4) With their attention and communication only about the wider context that has them relating the way they are (the observer or witness role).

Switch partners between rounds if you so desire.

Facilitator Instructions

It helps to demonstrate each with a co-facilitator.
· It sometimes helps to direct participants to name the connection between them and treat it as a separate being.
· You can use the format of, "who must I or you or us be to show up in this particular way" (example: "I'm feeling sad. I must trust you. Or this must be a safe place to be sad in. Or I might be the kind of person who feels sad when I drop deeply into connection.").

Attributions

Created by Sara Ness.

The Seems

This game plays with how shifting perspective can allow more range for connection, truth, and understanding to emerge. It usually takes 10-20 minutes, depending on how long you choose for each section to go on.

Instructions for Playing

Complete the phrase: "I seem . . ." popcorn-style for a few minutes. Anybody in the group can answer, either with how they think they seem to others or how they're feeling in the moment.

Switch to "You seem . . ." choosing a person in the group to project on with each share.

Switch to "We seem . . ." to notice how the group is together.

Switch to "The context is . . ." or "We are . . ." to speak to the wider frame defining why we are the way we are: physical space, demographics, why the group is together, etc. (Optional)

Switch to: "My context is..." identifying what is affecting each participant's experience in the moment.

Take shares.

Facilitator Instructions

"We seem" can be used as a game on its own, to track how the group's energy changes as it is spoken (and, for a great follow-up, try the sentence stem "What's not being spoken here is . . .").

Attributions

Created by Sara Ness for the Authentic Leadership Training

Try Me On

This is an edgy game, but highly insightful.

Instructions for Playing

Move around the room and think about the qualities of movement and being that make you who you are. Then stand in a circle with your group and answer the sentence stem "Who am I? I am...." For example, "I am comfortable and confident."

Once everyone has gone, take off as many pieces of clothing as feels comfortable and pass your clothing to the person on your left. Put on the clothing of the person who has passed you their clothes. To make this more private, you can divide participants into pairs and have them step into another room to exchange.

Then move around the room and see how it feels to be wearing someone else's clothing.

Come back to the circle and answer the sentence stem again, "Who am I? I am..." There can also be a few shares about how it feels to be inhabiting someone else's clothing, what it has taught you about yourself, what it is like to see how someone acts in your clothing. End there or keep passing the clothing to your left for a few more rounds.

Facilitator Instructions

You could ask people to wear swimsuits under their clothing to make it feel more comfortable to change clothing in front of others. It can also help to give people a sentence stem or way to get to know their partner a little before switching clothes.

Variations

- Changelings: Only two people from the group swap clothing. They then come back and introduce themselves: "I am..." and describe the traits and qualities they feel wearing the other's clothes. The swapper shares impact, then does the same introduction. Optional group shares, and two more people then choose to swap. Those who have already changed clothes embody the persona of the person whose clothes they're wearing for the rest of the game, and everyone can wander around afterwards interacting!

Attributions

Created by Abbi Jaffe of Authentic Burlington for an Authentic Leadership Training.

+Congregation of Believers

Setup
4-16 people

Time
30-60 minutes

The overall context for the game is to explore the group's relationship to a belief or perspective (here called "the article of faith") through an individual (the "I"). This takes inspiration from Internal Family Systems Theory (IFS).

Instructions for Playing

Volunteer or select roles for:
"Voice of God" = Facilitator
"The I" = Person bringing the Article of Faith
"Congregation of Believers" = All other participants

Round 1: Testify
"The I" has 5 minutes at the top to describe the article of faith, and how they've been experiencing it as of late. We are defining the article of faith as something that the person used to really believe in, and have lately been questioning (example: unconditional love, or working hard for money, the goodness of government etc.). This article should be general enough that everyone in the group has some relationship to it.

The I can answer: Why do I have faith in this? What thoughts, feelings or experiences make me doubt that article of faith?

As the I testifies, the Voice of God should start to name different perspectives that they are hearing, and write these on post-its or in Zoom chat.

Round 2: Converge
Each member of the Congregation of Believers then chooses a perspective to try on, i.e. "the communitarian," "the rebel," "the truth-seeker" or other roles that embody the different voices of doubt that emerged during The I's testimony. These perspectives are hereby known as "The Beliefs".

Participants may also suggest other Beliefs in their own relationship to this article of faith. It's okay to have more than one person holding a Belief at a time.

The Congregation of Believers puts on name tags / changes their Zoom name to their role.

Round 3: Debate
The Congregation of Believers then debate the Article of Faith, each arguing only for the perspective of their role. The I alone may represent any view at any time.

Believers can switch their Belief and join another Believer by changing their name tag /zoom name if they are convinced of that other Belief during the game, but they must first make at least 1 point in favor of their assigned Belief.

The Voice of God may intervene to modify the game at any time, in the following ways:

Cage Match:
Create a 2-minute "cage match" between two competing viewpoints.

Testify:
Compel a certain Believer, or the I, to speak just their view for a timed interval (good if a perspective or person isn't getting heard).

Echo:
Pause debate when something especially potent or charged has been said, and have each Believer repeat that word or phrase out loud, one at a time.

Wisdom Bath:
Allow something potent or charged to sink in for 30 seconds of silence.

Commandment:
Make a new rule of your choice.

The game completes when the Voice of God decides it is over (usually 15-30 minutes in). As a last round, The I shares any changes of view or insights they gained from seeing their Article of Faith played out. You can invite the same debrief from other group members as well.

Facilitator Notes

Use your Voice of God powers sparingly but directively during the game. You may also choose what type of God to be - jealous, benevolent, etc.

Attributions

Game created by Sara Ness and Kip Dooley during a Rising Practitioners lab

Feedback Games

Feedback Games

How often do we pause and open ourselves up to real, honest feedback about how we come across to others? Countless factors can gunk up the invisible pipes that flow connection energy back and forth between us and our friends, families, lovers, and colleagues. Hurtful experiences are left unsaid, gossip infects our communities, and folks with low EQ often walk around blindly acting on their impulses without understanding the impact of their Way Of Being – both good and bad.

Feedback games create a brave space for participants to get in on the joke of how they are seen and perceived. The flavor and intensity depends on how you choose to facilitate. Make sure to create space for integration and/or appreciation after these games.

Map of the Territory

· Truths and Withholds are classic short-form feedback games where we get to hear and clear the impact others have recieved from moments with us.

· Mirror of Perception, Kiss Kiss Diss, and Authentic Goodbye let others give honest reflections on how they see us in general.

· Doom Circle and Enrollment Game allow us to ask for feedback on a specific desire or life purpose, and see how others view our approach to that.

· Constellations is a comparison game where we see our role inside a group.

When to use Feedback Games:

· At the end of trainings and retreats

· With groups that have a shared experiences with each other, whether they be communities, teams, friend groups, or facilitation graduates

· As an alternative to traditional performance reviews or community clearings

Index

· *Truths
· Doom Circle
· *Witholds
· The Enrollment Game

· *Mirror of Perception
· Constellations
· Kiss Kiss Diss

**Truths

This is a great closure to any event, allowing us to share the little moments of impact that make up our experience with each other. In Austin, it's become a tradition to play at the end of every Games Night.

Instructions for Playing

In the full group, any person can share with another individual, or the group as a whole, "___(person's name), when you ____ (identify a particular, unarguable moment or experience), I felt ___(share an emotion)." Continue for however much time you have available or until the energy starts to fade. Optionally, check with the person to see if they are open for a Truth before sharing one.

Facilitator Instructions

You can opt to be more/less strict on how cleanly participants own their experience.

Variations

Withholds and Appreciations: Share for a withhold,
"When you [x action] I felt [x emotion] and what I would have preferred to happen is..."
Share for an appreciation,
"When you [x action] I felt [x emotion] and what I'm taking with me/what I appreciated about that is [x whatever you want]"

Partial Truths: Instead of saying "When you/ I felt" participants just say, "___(person's name), I felt ___(share an emotion)." Partial Truths was invented for an April Fools' Games Night, but ended up being a fascinating experience of intimate connection-shares, because the recipient of the truth often knew what the other was referring to even without context.

Attributions

From Authentic World. Partial Truths comes from Sara Ness and Josh Sabik of the Austin Love Juggernaut.

**Withholds

Withholds are things that we have left unsaid in a relationship or connection with another person. Sharing them regularly, before they build up, is the absolute best way I know to maintain relational health in a team, community, or relationship. These are a lifetime practice for me.

Instructions for Playing

Withholds can either be given in the full group, like Truths, or one-on-one at any time.

To share a withhold, first ask the person if they're open to it, and then set context for why you want to share.

For example:
"Sandra, may I share a withhold with you? We had a moment last week that really didn't feel good to me, and I've been holding a judgment about you since. I'd like to come back into connection."

Then, share whatever you haven't been saying with the person. Example:
"I was really pissed off when you overrode me in our planning meeting. I felt like I didn't matter to you, and then I had trouble participating in the rest of the event afterwards. How is that to hear from me? Did you notice that moment? What was happening for you?"

Give your partner time to respond, and continue going back and forth until you both feel complete.

Facilitator Instructions

How you share with someone will depend on your quality of connection with them, and your degree of comfort with discomfort. You may choose to give an unfiltered judgment or to own your experience using "I" statements. Whatever you choose, practice staying in connection throughout, and not distancing if the person you're sharing with gets triggered.

Attributions

Learned at The Integral Center

**Mirror of Perception

Setup
Full Group or
Breakout Groups

Time
10-20 minutes

How do our self-perceptions match up with the outside world? This game is one of the fastest ways I've found to see that. It could lead into longer games on perspective-taking, awareness, and/or self-love.

Instructions for Playing

Everyone in the group will get a chance to go for this game.
Pick a person to be reflected first (the "Focus").
For 1-3 minutes, invite members of the group to share qualities or attributes that they see in this person, popcorn-style. Others in the group can give twiddle fingers if they share that perception.

The "Focus" holds up a number of fingers from 1-5, with 1 being least and 5 most, to show how true that reflection feels in his/her own self-perception.

Then, for 1-3 minutes, invite the "Focus" to share qualities or attributes that they experience in themselves, and the rest of the group members give a 1-5 of how much they perceive that attribute in the Focus. Give a last minute for the Focus to share what they noticed playing the game.

Facilitator Instructions

- What I Think You Think of Me: Divide into pairs of A and B. A answers the sentence stem: "What I think you think of (or about) me is..." for 1-3 minutes. B holds up a number from 1-5, 1 being least accurate and 5 being most. Shares (or debrief with partner) and switch roles, then shares or pair debrief again, and rotate to a new partner.

Attributions

Invented by Sara Ness for Authentic Revolution's Boston Circling Training.

Kiss Kiss Diss

This game works best with people who are already familiar with each other.

Instructions for Playing

Form groups of 5-10. Designate one person (A) to go first.

The person 3 spots to A's left gives A a compliment, delivered with as much specificity as possible. "You're so generous!" is much less impactful than,

> "I've noticed you giving up your spot in several Games to a new participant, and standing out to watch, when we had odd numbers in the groups. I really admire that generosity - it's inspired me to be more aware of others' needs."

The person 2 spots to A's left also gives a compliment.

Finally, the person one spot to A's left gives a critique, something that A could work more on (in that person's opinion).

Optional: A shares impact.

Move the process one person to A's right and repeat, until everyone has received feedback

Notes

Invented by Ali Hussein of the Austin Love Juggernaut.

Doom Circle

Setup
Full Group

Time
20-45 min

This is a brutally honest feedback game, and is recommended for participants that are feeling well-resourced and groups that can be trusted to hold each other compassionately.

The magic is that this structure tends to bring up gems of difficult, personal feedback that people might otherwise never hear. It's also very good for coming to an understanding of how people view you.

Instructions for Playing

Set up the space in a way that allows everyone to feel confident and accepting of themselves, compassionately aligned with others, and ready to accept and examine difficult feedback.

All feedback is optional. Participants should feel the freedom to take what serves them and leave behind what does not.

One participant volunteers to be doom circled. They then have the opportunity to ask for a prompt and level of gentleness, if desired. Example:
"From what you understand to be my goals, what do you think I could be doing better or differently? I'd like a medium level of intensity - be honest, but try to own your experience and give me some space between shares to integrate."

Pick a scribe for the person being circled, taking notes so they can be fully present with the feedback they receive.

Then, other participants take turns giving feedback to the person being circled. Feedback should be given with care and respect, and for the benefit of the person in the middle, not for the person giving the feedback. Ways to do this include:

Speak from your own experience, and use "I" statements. "I've experienced you ignoring me" rather than "You are rude."
Where possible, make feedback specific and provide examples.
Remember your perspective is imperfect. Suggest, rather than demand changes. "If I were you, I might..." or "I would feel X if you...."

At the end of each share, the participant in the middle makes eye contact and says "Thank you." No further response is allowed.

When the person is done being Doom Circled (after a number of shares, allotted time, or when nobody else has feedback), they get 3 minutes to share their experience with the group, respond to any feedback they'd like, or say anything else they need to feel complete.

The group responds by thanking them for their courage.

Facilitator Instructions

Guide participants through practices of presence, acceptance, and gratitude while also considering human fallibility in self and others.

Take care when facilitating and monitoring the Doom circle. Pause as needed to allow the person being circled time to come down from peak emotional experiences and have a support system in place for participants. Make time for decompressing and integrating afterwards.

Variations

- Withhold Circle: The group doom circles a participant around withholds they may have for others in their life or in the group.

Attributions

Created by Telind Bench.

+The Enrollment Game

Setup
Triads

Time
20-30 min

Enrollment is what helps people understand and want to do what you want them to do. We often do this badly, trying to convince people without giving them enough information either about why we want something or what, exactly, we're expecting from them. Bad examples: "Can we talk?" "Can you help me on this project?" "We need to fix this." "Go vote!"

To enroll people well, we need to give them the what, the how, and the why of what we want. We have to engage them from both their desire and our own.

Instructions for Playing

Think of something you really want - something you genuinely desire, not just aspire to (i.e. if you got it, you would be excited and/or motivated, not confused or overwhelmed). Consider: how could 2 strangers help you accomplish that desire? For example:

> "I want to become a full-time musician. I'd like y'all to help plan and throw me a fundraiser, and donate to it too!"

> "I'm looking for a partner. I want y'all to interview me on my best qualities, and then recommend people who might like me!"

You are going to try using the what, the why, and the how to enroll two other people into helping you achieve your goal. Just so you know, this is a practical game. If you enroll these people, you can hold them to doing the thing!

In your triad, choose an Earth, a Wind, and a Fire.

Fires, share for 2 minutes about something you want from your partners, giving the what, why, and how. Try to enroll them!

Winds and Earths, give some feedback for 3 minutes. What more information, intention, or context would you need to be a hell yes to any or all parts of this?

Fires, you have 3 more minutes to try to enroll, getting feedback throughout. If your partners are enrolled, coordinate details with them!

Earths and Winds, what do you appreciate about the bravery or skill of your Fire? Share that with them for 2 minutes. Then, switch roles.

Attributions

Sara Ness of Authentic Revolution, modified from an Integral Center game

**Constellations

Setup
Full Group

Time
45 minutes

This is an incredible exercise for showing members their effect (or lack of it) on the group, and can lead into generative energy around clearing withholds, creating projects, and honest self-reflection. This can be played for fun with a new group with more surface-level prompts, but is an edgy game in any situation because there will be people not chosen.

Instructions for Playing

Form a large circle. One person will act as facilitator and give the prompts.

When a prompt is given, Everyone should look around the circle, find the person for whom that prompt is most true in their opinion, go over, and put a hand on that person's shoulder. Only choose one person to touch at a time. If you choose not to play for a prompt, you can put your hands behind your head, and that means that you will neither pick someone nor are available to be picked. Constellations will form and may move around the room as each person makes their decision.

When the room has settled, pause and look around at where the focal points are, and how it feels having your hand on somebody and having hands (or not) on you. Also take note of any connections you may want to make later on based on this. Then everyone returns to a circle for another prompt. After several of these, you could open up for suggestions from the group.

Example prompts:
 The person in the group that you trust the most
 The person in the group that you respect the most
 The person in the group that you feel least connected to
 The person you'd most like to get drunk with
 The person in the group that you are most attracted to (or find most beautiful)
 The person in the group that you think contributes most to this community
 The person in the group that you think was most popular in high school
 Somebody you want to get to know better
 Somebody you have a withhold for
 Somebody that you want to work with on a project

Attributions

Sara first encountered this game at the Toronto Feel. Connect.
Expand. retreat, and has used it many times since at community gatherings and staff retreats.

Curiosity
Games

Curiosity Games

Curiosity games are the perfect introduction to Authentic Relating. They can be played within formal events, but are just as good to introduce during hangouts, on dates, and as icebreakers in team meetings.

These games are a fast and effective route to diving a few layers beneath the surface of everyday conversations by leaning into our genuine curiosity. You can also use these to subtly train people to have better conversations with each other, by creating space for a dialogue between the aliveness of certain discussion topics vs. more boring ones.

Map of the Territory

· I Don't Know About You and Pandora's Box (along with the Curiosity Tapas variant of Curiosity) help us see possibilities for what we can be curious about.

· The "Google" Game and Inception move into question asking, but with low creativity necessary. These first two sections help participants who struggle with curiosity.

· Curiosity, Cartography, and Hot Seat give simple formats for asking questions on a turn-taking basis.

· Interrupting and Following Aliveness and Question Ambassador allow the questioner to be more selfish with their curiosity.

When to use Curiosity Games:

· Early in a session, games night, work meeting, date, or casual hangout
· As a warm-up for deeper empathy games
· To create a quick layer of interconnectedness and safety among the group
· To invite participants into engaging and deep conversations at their level of comfort

Index

**Truths

A great way to get ready to play Curiosity, and to open up work or personal relationships that have gone on for long enough that the members have lost some curiosity about each other.

Instructions for Playing

Partners choose an A and a B. A begins by saying things they don't know about B, for 1-2 minutes. For example, "I don't know when the last time you talked to your parents was." "I don't know what you think about illegal drug use." Then either segue into Curiosity or switch.

Attributions

Developed by Scott Gregory.

+Pandora's Box

Setup
Pairs/Triads/small groups

Time
25 min

This mashup of 3 games offers an opportunity to get in touch with what has our curiosity in the moment and what you want/need others to be curious about in you. A big part of our curiosity of others and revealing ourselves is noticing, putting attention on what arises around us, or triggers us, as well as what we are needing/longing for others to be curious about us.

Instructions for Playing

For 4 rounds, share each time with 1-2 short sentences or a few words. Each round, go around the circle twice.

Round 1: "Inside of me, I notice...." (go around twice)
Round 2: "Outside of me, I notice....." (go around twice)
Round 3: "If you really knew me, you would be curious about/that..."
Round 4: "To really know me, it is important that you are curious about/that..."

Facilitator Instructions

Do this round-robin or popcorn style for 4 rounds in the full group, responding twice for each round. Can be played in dyads or triads - adjust time accordingly.

To vary the game, you can change the sentence stems for different theme nights, or add impact sharing by listeners.

Attributions

From Dianne Zomper of Authentic Houston

**The "Google" Game

Setup
Pairs or Breakout Groups

Time
10-20 min

In Authentic Relating Games and Circling we often tend to emphasize and dive deep into vulnerable, present-moment connection, but we don't actually know each other in other ways. This game is to round that out. While not as deep, it can be very nourishing and also essential for community building.

Fun note on the history of this game: I was on a 2nd date and the guy I was with was moving really fast (in other words, all over me). I had asked him to slow down and told him I wanted to know him more and connect more physically out of a feeling of personal intimacy. I was not getting through to him. I'm not sure how this idea was generated in that moment but I peeled him off my face and said "let's play a game" - I had no idea what would come out of my mouth next. "If I were to Google you and Italy, what would I find". We started to get to know each other more and the Google Game was born. PS - it is a fun game to play on road trips too!"~Amy

Instructions for Playing

Direct each person to "Google" another for a few minutes, by saying "Jen, if I were to Google you and (puppies), what would I find?" Jen then answers with her association with puppies - maybe a story that feels relevant or a memory or just her feelings about puppies. Do not answer as if this were a real informational inquiry: the "Google search" is searching into the answerer's memory and associations.

This game can be set around a theme, where all the questions/Google searches are relevant to a particular topic/concept. For example, "If I were to Google you and "shame" what would I find? If I were to Google you and "desire" what would I find?"

Variations

- Click and Zoom: After a first round of the Google Game, try a second round where the questioner can "double-click" things they found interesting in what their partner shared. For example: A says "Google 'Sara' and 'love triangles." B (Sara): "The first thing that comes up is a memory of a complicated affair I had while exploring polyamory..." A: "Double-click 'polyamory'." B: "I was polyamorous for 3 years..."

Attributions

From Amy Silverman of The Connection Movement (NY)

Inception ("What's that like?")

Setup
Pairs

Time
7-12 min

The goal of this game is to refine and expand on an experience, becoming aware of the layers of emotion occurring at any given time.

Instructions for Playing

In pairs, choose an A and a B.

A shares what they are feeling or experiencing in the moment, or what's on top for them.

B asks variants of, "What's that like?" or "What's it like to feel that?" B can also notice dissonance: "What's it like to feel sad and be smiling at the same time?"

Go for 2-5 minutes, then switch roles.

Facilitator Instructions

Encourage participants to really stick to the format. It will seem restrictive but, like lifting weights, this builds particular muscles of awareness and curiosity. This game led to surprising breakthroughs for many participants, and didn't require a facilitator to be present in the pairs.

Attributions

Developed by Jordan Myska Allen of Circle Anywhere for use in a circling class series.

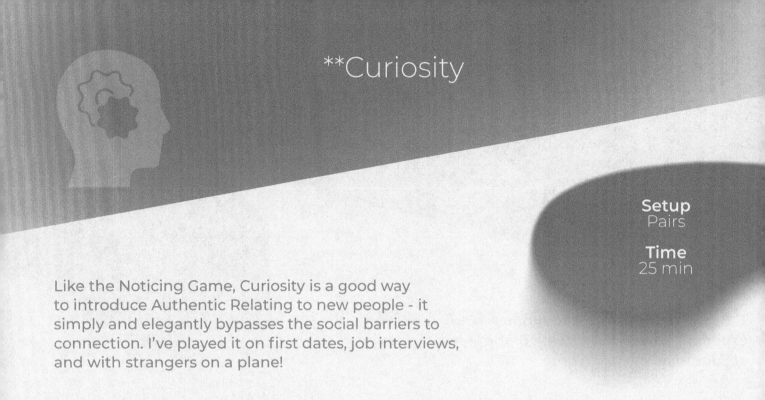

**Curiosity

Setup
Pairs

Time
25 min

Like the Noticing Game, Curiosity is a good way to introduce Authentic Relating to new people - it simply and elegantly bypasses the social barriers to connection. I've played it on first dates, job interviews, and with strangers on a plane!

Instructions for Playing

Pair up, either at random or choosing a partner about whom you are curious. Decide who will be A and B.

A's have 5 minutes to ask B whatever they want, provided that they feel really, genuinely curious to know the answer to their question. B's can answer or decline to respond to any question. At the end of the time, B's get a chance to give a minute of feedback to A on how they felt about the questions, including if there was anything they wished had been asked or anything that really struck them.

A resumes questioning for 3 minutes.

At the end of the time, A gives a "gift" to B of three sentence stems:
  · "My first impression of you was. . ."
  · "I felt you the most when . . ."
  · "What I really get about you is . . ."
  · (Optional: B responds with emotional impact for a minute, or shares "What I WANT you to get about me is...").

Facilitator Instructions

Try the game with different timings, different pairings, and different sentence stems at the end. I like using "The adventure I'd like to go on with you is..."

Variations

- Speed Curiosity: This is best played in two lines, or with an inner and outer circle, so switches can happen quickly. Partners only have 30 seconds or 1 minute to ask. Go with the first thing you feel really curious about when the person across from you sits down. You can either have A's asking every time until the circle has gone around once, and then B's ask; or switch off A's and B's asking questions quickly. This can act as an authentic improv game, helping people to turn off their filters, and also to notice what things they generally tend to be curious about and what things about them others tend to find curious.

- Curiosity Tapas: You can either play this to start with, as curiosity calibration, or instead of the feedback round. A's ask questions for 1 minute, and B's (instead of answering) shares their interest in answering the question by holding up a number of fingers, 1-5. 1 is "Eh...I guess I could talk about that, if it makes you happy..." and 5 is "Can I respond yet??" After a minute, resume the game, with more enthusiastic interactions guaranteed.

- Curiosity 2.0: Person A and person B go back and forth, continuously asking questions. With each question, they up the ante, asking a deeper, more specific or vulnerable question around the same line. This game can also be played as a Hot Seat or a quad (played the same with a witnessing pair that may ask clarifying questions, allowing time for pairs to switch roles).

- Curiosity Empathy Mashup: Person A will first have 1-2 minutes to ask questions. Instead of answering, B's will hold up fingers, rating their interest in the question (1 being low, 5 being high). Afterwards, A's will have the opportunity to ask one question based on their feedback. B's speak to this question for 2-3 minutes, with person A now only listening. Person A will have 1-2 minutes to repeat back what they heard with as little interpretation as possible. B's may then clarify or continue speaking for 1-2 minutes. Lastly, A's have a minute to share a gift, such as what they think they get about person B now, or where they felt them the most. Switch roles.

Attributions

Developed by Authentic World. Speed Curiosity, Curiosity Tapas, and Curiosity 2.0 variations come from the Austin Love Juggernaut. Curiosity Empathy Mashup is from Shaina List of Authentic Relating Toronto.

Cartography

Setup
Pairs

Time
20-30 min

Cartography is like Curiosity turned sideways. One player gets to "sketch a map" of another person's mind by identifying as many interesting landmarks as possible. Focus on the breadth of the landscape, not the depth of one feature. Then hand them the map and let them fill in more details to discover themselves more clearly or completely.

Instructions for Playing

Pick an A and B.

For 7 minutes, B explores A's mind by posing serious questions about whether A would make various choices. A answers truthfully, giving a condition if necessary, i.e.
"Yes, if _____ were true."

Question structures are hypothetical, i.e.
· "Would you ever...?"
· "Would you rather...?"
· "Would you like...?"
· "Would you like to....?"

B's goal is to learn as many things about A's preferences and identity as possible.

For 1-2 minutes, B shares with A, "What I think I get about you is..."

Attributions

This game was created by David Staab of the Austin Love Juggernaut.

**Hot Seat

Setup
Breakout Groups

Time
15-45 min

This game is always a favorite for its rapid depth and boldness, and brings a lot of energy to the room. Consider ending any version of this game with group shares of "What I get about you is..." and/or "I felt you the most when..." to help ground the experience.

Instructions for Playing

Designate a chair as the "hot seat." Folks can volunteer to sit on the hot seat, and choose their desired level of intensity (mild, medium, or spicy). The rest of the group asks probing questions of the person on the hot seat, with depth / intensity according to the level of spiciness.

Facilitator Instructions

Instruct the group to ask interested, not interesting questions - the difference is that interested questions keep the focus on the person answering, while interesting questions pull the focus back to the questioner. Give it about 4-10 minutes per person, and aim to end when you feel the high note has been hit. "...and I'll take you off the hot seat there."

Variations

- Thank you: At any point during the response to their question, the questioner can say "Thank you" which is a signal for the person on the hot seat to STOP TALKING - even mid-sentence. This ensures that the hot seat inhabitant doesn't ramble, and helps keep the heat up.

- Inquisition: This version was developed after a frustratingly slow and thoughtful Hot Seat round. The shock value of Inquisition means that the person on the Hot Seat will often find themselves being improvisationally truthful. Instructions: form a close, standing circle around the person in the "hot seat", who is seated. Give 3 minutes for rapid-fire questioning, where anybody has thank-you power whether or not they asked the question, and the standing circle can poke the middle person if they don't answer quickly enough (if the person in the middle agrees to physical contact. Or the people on the outside can snap their fingers, if the middle person does not agree to physical contact). The person in the middle can refuse to answer questions they don't want to respond to, but must respond right away. If you want, you can offer them the ability to make a request at the end of the circle, or offer them a group hug.

· Spotlight: This is designed to be a group version of the Curiosity game, with the intention of extending positive regard and getting one person's world. Choose one person to be in the Spotlight. The rest of the group can ask that person questions, but must raise their hands and wait for the facilitator to call on them before asking. The person asking a question can say 'Thank you" to indicate that they are finished listening (this isn't a hard cut-off, but it is a nudge to wrap it up). Direct the participants to keep the Spotlight on the subject (ask interested not interesting questions), follow the rabbit hole (preference for what's arising in the moment, and where the most juice is), and ask honest questions (no embedded assertions which might not be true).

Then the askers, popcorn-style, answer the question "When did you feel a lot with X?" for about 3 minutes. After that, tell the group: "Now you get to share your new understanding of X with him/her." This is riskier territory: they might feel profoundly seen, or they might feel not seen. So again popcorn-style answer the question "What do you really get about X?" (Give this some more time, and end on a high note if you can.) Tell the participant, "Your spotlight is complete".

· Dead Seat: Imagine that the person on the Hot Seat has died, and is talking about their life as it has been, or as they see it now. The group asks questions about their former self and their relationship to who they were.

· Hot Mic: As breakout groups or full group, participants stand in a circle. An instrumental beat is played in the background, such as live drumming or strumming. Lights dimmed if desired. One person holds the mic (or banana, stick, etc) and responds to questions from the group for 5-7 minutes. No rhyming experience necessary, as responses can be given with singing, rapping, or spoken word.

Attributions

This game dates back to Vic Baranco and the Morehouse Community in the 1970s, and is sourced from Authentic World in this form. Variations: Spotlight comes from Michael McDonald of Relational Alchemy, Dead Seat is from Micah Sutton of Austin, Hot Mic is from Naveed Heydari of Authentic Denver, and Inquisition was developed by the Austin community.

+Interrupting and Following Aliveness

Setup
Pairs

Time
15 min

Interrupting is one of the hardest and most crucial skills for having interesting or difficult conversations. So, we're going to practice it!

Instructions for Playing

Choose a partner A and a partner B.

Partner A, talk about something relatively boring that happened for you this week.
Partner B, at least every 30 seconds, find a way to interrupt (you can have a timer ready for this). After interrupting, ask the other person a question about something you're really interested about. You can use these sentence stems: "What I'm really curious about is..." or "Can you say more about..."?

Take around 4 minutes to interrupt and get curious, and then 1.5 minutes to debrief.
What was it like to interrupt, and especially to be interrupted? Switch roles.

Attributions

Sara Ness and Geof Krum for the Art of Difficult Conversations course

Question
Ambassador

Setup
Full Group

Time
15-30 min

This game allows participants to create intimate mini-surveys of how multiple people feel on a question of their choice.

Instructions for Playing

Count everybody off as A's and B's. B's move their chairs to the inside of the room, in front of an A, and then scoot in until the backs of all B's chairs are touching to form a circle in the center. A's scoot in to be right in front of a B, creating two concentric circles. Everybody then chooses a sentence stem that they want to ask for the duration of the game.

A's ask B's, who respond for 1 minute, then B's ask A's for 1 min. Then the outer circle rotates one (or two) people to their left. Each person will always be asking the same stem and receiving a different one. In terms of rotation, you can play with how many spaces people move over so participants can't watch who they will end up in front of (especially important in the blindfolded version).

Facilitator Instructions

To help people choose a question to ask, you can offer some examples of sentence stems - deep, fun, or both. Other ideas:
  · Make up a game to help people choose their stems, eg. A's help B's explore what sentence stems they might choose and why (Empathy or Distillation could be good for this)
  · Pairs take 2 minutes to talk over their thoughts with each other
  · Each person closes their eyes and thinks of a stem alone

Variations

  · Blindfolded: After each partner chooses a stem, the inner circle (B's) put on blindfolds. A's ask their stem, for 1 minute, and then rotate. B's will always be answering (until the sides switch and A's put on the blindfolds, and B's can ask), but will not know who is asking the question. Remind A's that their partners will not know who is asking, so they can really lean into their edge on the question they choose to ask; remind B's that they can be honest without repercussion (and with confidentiality available by request).

Attributions

From the Austin Love Juggernaut.

Empathy Games

Empathy Games

Good communication comes down to a few core skills: active listening, questioning our stories about others, reflecting what we hear – and practicing empathy.

Empathy games are perfect for emotional intelligence training. They break down the ability to empathize and have deep conversations into their constituent building blocks. As well as developing EQ skills, these are some of the best games to connect people on a soul level. Participants will feel understood, and they will learn more about the conversation dynamics that can bring that aliveness back into their everyday lives.

Map of the Territory

· Empathy and Storytelling Reflection invite us to repeat someone's words and way of being back to them, to see themselves more clearly and help us understand them.

· I've Felt That and Rooms of the Heart prompt us to reflect on the feelings and experiences we share with others.

· Ducklings, If I Were You... and Frustration Station actually put us in the role of another person, experiencing their perspective from the inside in.

When to use Empathy Games:

· In the middle to late part of a session
· For emotional intelligence or conflict resolution trainings
· In couples' coaching
· When you want all participants to have a chance to feel seen and understood

Index

**Empathy

Setup
Pairs

Time
15 min

One of our most simple, deep, and reliable exercises.

Instructions for Playing

In pairs, take a few seconds to make silent eye contact and get present with each other. Pick an A and B.

A has 3 minutes to share something that's on their heart, while B listens actively.
B has 1 min to share exactly what they heard, with as little interpretation as possible.
A then reiterates, adds, or clarifies their share for 3 minutes.
B shares what they felt listening to the whole process, and/or what they get about A for 2 minutes.
Pair debrief and group sharebacks.

Facilitator Instructions

You can optionally give participants a prompt or sentence stem to play this game around. Depending on the group culture - especially in more professional or European groups - you may need to give more time for each round.

Variations

- Empathy can also be played in groups of three, with C acting as a second reflector after A's shares.

- Empathetic Conversation: A's speak for 3 min on something alive for them.
  B's listen, then reflect and ask: "What else?" or "Is that it?"
  A's continue speaking for another 3 minutes, while B's imagine: "What I think I get [about this, about you] is____. Is that true? What is true for you?"
  Last, Bs empathize for 3 min: share where they find resonance in their own life or experience, or share emotional impact.
  Shares, switch, and play again.

Attributions

Developed by the Austin Love Juggernaut, adapted from Marshall Rosenberg's Nonviolent Communication work.

Storytelling Reflection

A creative, rewarding way to explore expression and empathy.

Instructions for Playing

Form groups of 4-5 people.

One person takes 3-4 minutes to stand in front of their small group and act out a story or a response to a prompt, e.g.

· "Your first time"
· "A part of you that feels broken"
· "Who you were that has changed"
· "What you feel like right now"

They can use both words and body motions.

Then, the others in their group have 3-5 minutes total to physically/verbally mirror parts of the share that impacted them, and then share what they got about the actor. Switch to the next person until all have gone.

Facilitator Instructions

Demo this game vulnerably to help encourage participants to do the same.

Attributions

Discovered at the Integral Center. However, I believe it is taken from the Zegg Forum, which plays out a similar scenario in larger groups.

I've Felt That

It's amazing how, regardless of how strange the combination of emotions seems, someone always seems to have felt it. This game can bring about some deep empathy and unexpected stories.

Instructions for Playing

Divide into pairs and find a comfortable space to share.

For the first round, A will speak 3 emotions they felt at one time in their life. No context or stories will be given. B will then ponder on these emotions, and share a story of a time in their life they felt those same emotions.

A may then share what they learned, impacts, or what felt similar or different.

Reverse roles, allowing B to share 3 emotions. Optional sharebacks.

Variations

· Feelings Wheel: Get into groups of 2-4. Each group gets a copy of the **Feelings Wheel** (search for it on Google). One person chooses three emotions off the wheel, then the other(s) can tell a story of a time they felt those emotions.

Attributions

Created by Zachary Robison of Authentic Houston with variation from Shane Orton of the Austin Love Juggernaut.

Rooms of the Heart

Setup
Pairs, Triads, or Quads

Time
20-40 minutes

This game is meant to explore our relationship with different parts or "rooms" of ourselves.

Instructions for Playing

Choose a person A in your group.

A shares about a "room" in themselves: an aspect they contain, like a "playful room" or a "work room", or any room they choose.

You may preface this with a sentence stem like, "If my heart had different rooms, the one I use the most is..." The group may become more curious about person A's room and ask questions, getting more of person A's world and room, for 4 minutes. Person A also shares how it is to have the other members of the group with them in this room.

Then, for 4 minutes, the other group members share back to person A what their versions of that room are in their own lives (ex. "I have a playful room too, which is like yours in these ways, and it's also...")

Optional shares of impact in the group, and switch to the next person.

Notes

Created by Sara Ness and Jennifer Ott.

Ducklings

Setup
Breakout Groups

Time
15 min-1 hour

This game gives the "Mama Duck" a chance to be fully witnessed "in vivo" and to learn how others interpret or see deeply into their behaviors. "Ducklings" get to practice this insight by guessing at the private experiences of someone they're watching.

Instructions for Playing

One player becomes the Mama Duck, other players are Ducklings. (These are just titles. You're not pretending to be ducks. And "Mama Duck" is gender-neutral here. Choose whatever title they prefer, or just use the person's name and pronoun.) Ducklings follow Mama around the space (a room, a building, a city block, etc) witnessing Mama Duck's actions and interpreting them to understand Mama's motivations and values. Ducklings verbalize what they see along with their interpretations of it. Example:

> Mama Duck walks to an outdoor spigot and drinks from it, then splashes some on a Duckling. Another duckling narrates aloud, "Mama finds a source of water and drinks liberally with no concern for potability. Mama splashes one of us to invite us to play with her!" Mama then sits on the ground and starts to draw in the dirt. Ducklings: "Mama becomes introspective." "Mama doesn't actually want to play with us."

Attributions

Developed by David Staab of the Austin Love Juggernaut.

If I Were You...

If I were REALLY YOU, I would have done EXACTLY WHAT YOU DID. That's what being you means. This game helps to explore that perspective.

Instructions for Playing

In pairs, pick an A and a B.

A has 5-7 minutes to tell B's about an experience from A's own life - perhaps a time they felt scared or endangered, or something that's been stuck in their mind the last few days. B's can inquire more about the experience because they will be coming back to the full circle to tell A's story, so they should be greedy and lead the inquiry to get what they need to act as storyteller.

After each round, asker-B's close their eyes and reflect on the story as if it was their own experience in their own life.

After both partners have shared, bring everybody back to the full circle (or divide into quads, if you have a group of more than 6-8 people), and give each B's 2 to 3 minutes to retell the heart of their partner's experience in the first person as their own story.

Then open it up to questions for B's (2 to 3 minutes for each question round). Let B's know that they don't have to know the real answer to respond; they can imagine and assume their partner's experience.

After the story and question round, ask A's:
    How was it to hear your story told?
    In what ways did you feel seen and gotten?
    Is there anything missing for you or anything that you want to add?

Facilitator Instructions

David Bollt (the creator) says: "Running this game felt more like a weekend deep dive than a games night: there were stories of abuse, near death, childhood trauma and other profound life altering experiences. The biggest leap for people in relating seems to be taking a genuine second position. Often people say "If I were you I WOULD HAVE"... which is basically saying "if I were ME in your situation."

Attributions

Developed by David Bollt of Asheville, NC.

**Frustration Station

Setup
Pairs

Time
30-45 min

This is an intense game, but very useful for helping people discover how to work with (or at least better understand) people in their life that they struggle to be authentic with.

Instructions for Playing

A thinks of someone they have trouble relating to in conversation (hereafter referred to as "the Jerk") and embodies this person.

B initiates an authentic conversation with A, and A responds as the Jerk. B delves into the depths of their authentic relating skills and converses with the Jerk for 3 minutes.

Afterwards, A and B exchange impact for 1 minute. A shares a few sentences of information to help B embody the Jerk. (ex: "It's my dad, and he's a therapist. He genuinely wants to connect with me but doesn't quite know how. When I was pretending to be him I felt trapped and confused.")

B embodies the Jerk this time. A initiates conversation and B responds as the Jerk for 3 minutes. A and B once again exchange impact for 1 minute. Switch roles.

Take full group sharebacks.

Facilitator Instructions

Since there are a lot of steps, you may want to introduce the Instructions for Playing throughout the game rather than all at the start.

Some people respond badly to calling their difficult conversationalist "Jerk", so you can choose a different name if you want.

Attributions

From Annabeth Novitski of the Austin Love Juggernaut, created in collaboration with Sara Ness during an Authentic Leadership and Facilitation Training.

Movement and Touch Games

Movement and Touch Games

Studies have shown that consensual touch lowers cortisol levels, strengthens our immune systems, deepens bonds and even reduces drug cravings.

Movement and touch games can destigmatize the shame and murkiness that underscores many participants' relationship to touch. They give open/experienced participants the opportunity to give and receive love through embodiment. And they give more reserved participants the opportunity to practice boundaries and notice their comfort in moving, touching, being touched, and being seen.

ALSO, many of these games are just plain fun!

Map of the Territory

· Stick Game and Moving Interaction are playful ways to explore contact.

· Blind Desire, Reach Out Touch Me, and Progressive Touch slow us down to experience our actual responses and desires within safe physical connection.

· Witnessed Movement, Touch My Elbow, and What's Here Now? allow us to explore touch and movement through the reflection of others' hands and eyes.

· Unconditional Hugs and Angel Walk use touch as a form of appreciation.

When to use Movement and Touch Games:

· With more embodied groups like ecstatic dance, cuddle parties, and play parties

· To build group connection in the body, after creating safety with some intellectual and/or emotional games like those earlier in this manual

· As a sequence to end a session or retreat with lots of love

Index

· *Stick Game
· Witness Movement
· Moving Interaction
· Touch My Elbow
· Blind Desire

· *What's Here Now?
· Reach Out, Touch Me
· *Unconditional Hugs
· Progressive Touch
· *Angel Walk

**Stick Game

Setup
Pairs

Time
10 min

Materials
Sticks about
1 ft long. Pencils
can be used in a
pinch.

I love playing this game at the end of a night. It's both fun, and can be an insightful exploration of our relationship to leading and following/ surrender and control.

Instructions for Playing

Divide into pairs.

Each pair gets a short stick (4-6 inches long - pencils or even touching index fingers will work in a pinch).

Each member of the pair puts their index finger on one end of the stick. Move around the room together without dropping the stick. If partners drop the stick, they must pick it up only using the tips of their index fingers.

After a few minutes, switch off who is leading and who is following.

Shuffle pairs, then play again, but without a defined lead or follow.

Facilitator Instructions

Try asking after one round if any pairs have not dropped their stick once, and give those pairs two sticks to make it harder!

This is good to play with background music.

Variations

· Double Blind: Partners play with their eyes closed.

· Twister: Partners balance the stick on nose, elbow, or other body parts.

Attributions

Developed by Authentic World.

Moving Interaction

Very effective in helping a large group of participants feel connected to each other, or for waking groups up after a break. This game usually ends itself after about 10 minutes.

Instructions for Playing

Participants mill around the room.

When you come into contact with somebody else, or meet eyes, interact with that person in some way - with a sound, a gesture, or a touch.

Then move on and interact with another person. If a participant does not want to interact physically in a way another participant offers, they can give a silent "namaste" (hands together in front of the heart) and offer a different form of interaction, or move on.

Facilitator Instructions

Demo with animal noises, contact improvisation, hugs, leapfrog, fake battles, deep eye-gazing, etc.

Attributions

Invented by Sara Ness.

Blind Desire

This game is deeply grounding, and good to play at the start of events or after a break to help participants drop into presence and connection.

Instructions for Playing

With closed eyes pay attention to your sensations, then to what your body wants. Start letting your body follow its desires - moving or not moving, fast or slow, just a toe or stretching everything - without sound, without moving out of place in the group, and with eyes still closed.

Then, start letting your desire lead you to move through the space, if you want to move. If you come into contact with another person, move away from that touch, staying attuned to your own sensations and following your own pleasure in however you are choosing to move.

After a few minutes, start forming contact with others, - still nonverbal and with eyes closed- if that feels good, with the invitation to "create experiences for each other".

Let that go for a few minutes and then as the energy begins to rise, choose to share one word with the person/people you're interacting with that describes the feeling of this connection.

Finally, everyone opens their eyes and looks around. After a minute or two see where you're at and what you've been doing, and enjoy the nonverbal closeness.

Move into a full-group circle and take shares.

Facilitator Instructions

Guide the experience by reading the instructions out as suggestions/directions.

Attributions

Developed by Sara Ness for the Texas Authentic Relating Retreats.

Reach Out, Touch Me

Setup
Pairs

Time
5-10 Min

This game is meant to slow down connection and allow participants to focus on what a very simple interaction feels like in their body.

Instructions for Playing

In seated pairs. Play with connection, nonverbally, while only allowing your fingertips to touch . . . then hands . . . then hands and arms (a minute or more for each mode of connection). Experiment with having eyes closed or open. Debrief.

Facilitator Instructions

Facilitated correctly, it can act as a powerful connect-to-self and connect-to-other. If you want a longer or more guided version of the game, try "Progressive Touch".

Progressive Touch

Setup
Pairs

Time
45 min

"I find touch to be a universal means of self-expression and connection. [This game explores] progressive touch – noticing how touch feels at progressive levels of connection, [developing an] internal sense – quiet mind, looking inward, feeling outward; and...without words communicating on a soul level." ~ Sharon

Instructions for Playing

Find a partner, either someone you want to work with or someone you're curious about. Once you've introduced yourselves, follow the steps below, allowing about a minute for each action.

- Close your eyes and breathe. Try to synchronize breath with your partner for a minute.
- Now, open your eyes – gaze with your partner, keep breathing.
- Bring hands together as close as you can without touching.
- Close your eyes again and try to keep your hands close without touching. If you touch, adjust as needed.
- Then surrender to the touch – but only touch fingertips, eyes closed.
- Open your eyes and make contact, still only touching fingertips.
- Then slowly allow your whole hand to touch: first fingers, palms, then forearms to elbows if you can reach.
- For 2 minutes, contact dance with hands/arms.
- Then lower your hands and just make eye contact.

Choose a partner to be partner A (longest hair, etc).
- Partner A sculpts partner B's face with your hands, without touching them.
- Partner B – follow partner A's hands with your face and eyes. If their hand goes out of view, follow the other hand, or wait for it to return. 5 minutes of hand-face practice. Half way through – if both partners would like to - move to touching face, hair and shoulders.
- Switch partners for 5 minutes. Then hands down.
- Deep eye contact, non verbal for 1 minute.

10-15 minutes (depending on group feel.)
- Stand up. Keep eyes open but turned down to the floor.
- Hands at your side. Walk around in a mingle style, making contact with others as you pass them.
- A few minutes in, allow hands to interact, while keeping appropriate boundaries. Allow hands to explore others in passing, brushing hands, arms, shoulders, head, etc.
- Linger with a person, or move around as you are called to do. Try to keep eyes closed, opening if needed to reconnect with the group.
- Then, for a minute, stop where you are, view the people around you, breathe in the connection.

Find your original partner. For 2 minutes, share impact back and forth:
- "Connecting with you, I feel_____"
- 2 minutes: "What I get about you now is _____"
- 2 minutes: "What I get about me now is _____"

Take 5-10 minutes for group shares and close.

Facilitator Instructions

Explain and demonstrate. Read the steps to guide the group through the experience.

Notes

From Sharon Swedlow of the Austin Love Juggernaut.

Witnessed Movement

Setup
Pairs

Time
10-15 minutes

This is powerful and beautiful as a presence practice.

Instructions for Playing

Pair up and spread out over the space so you can move in the spot without hitting each other.

One member of each pair (A) closes their eyes and does whatever movement they want. The other member (B) observes, with strong focus and intent, trying to feel into how it is to be A dancing. Witnesses can feel free to somewhat mimic their mover's moves, if it is in service of feeling them more (not to co-create or take over).

At about 5 min, A's come to rest.

Share impact - first B sharing, then A - then switch.

Variations

- Empathy Dance: After about 3 minutes of watching, the witnesses begin joining the dance, by assisting and enhancing the mover's movements. Witnesses should not personally initiate any movement. The mover's eyes should remain closed. Witnesses see how much they can be in the mover's world, sharing and enjoying who this person is through feeling their dance with them. Stop after 3-5 minutes and share in pairs, then in the group.
  Optional:
  After both partners have gone, co-create a dance of shared reality. You can also dance together at the beginning and then at the end, to experience the change.

Attributions

This is an old game whose antecedents I don't know,
but which I've seen played in many places.

Touch
My Elbow

Setup
Pairs

Time
10-15 minutes

"This is a simple, fast, and fun game encouraging physical interaction. It is about respecting yourself by making requests for something you want and by saying no if you don't want to honor someone else's requests." ~Walt

Instructions for Playing

Divide into partners. The person with the longest sleeves goes first.

In this game you and a partner are going to take turns asking to be touched in a specific place. The request should be fairly specific in the form of "I would like my <blank> to be touched". Your partner either complies by lightly touching that spot for you, or they decline.

Like the game Twister, once you touch a spot continue to do so until you need to move that hand to touch another spot. If your partner declines to touch you somewhere, you are obligated to touch that spot on yourself.

If you are a bit squeamish about being physically touched, you can indicate a piece of clothing like a sleeve or a shoe.

Take turns requesting spots. If you and your partner are a little more comfortable or adventurous, remember, you don't have to touch with your hand.

Play for a few minutes, then take shares.

Variations

- As You Like It: partners can request the kind of touch they'd like on each location (light, heavy, gliding, etc.) after initial contact is made.

Attributions

Created by Walt Stein of the Austin Love Juggernaut.

**What's Here Now?

Setup
Pairs

Time
20-30 minutes

Instructions for Playing

Divide into pairs.

B lies down if comfortable, then brings A's hand anywhere on their body.

A rests their hand on B's body in pure, simple witness presence, with a relaxed hand exactly where it has been guided. A does not move the hand.

A can begin to inquire to B, "What's here now?" B answers at the level of sensation and/or emotion.

A can continue to ask "What's here now?" at intervals of a few seconds to a minute, in the same spot multiple times, as things arise and pass. Feel into the space between questions, and then ask again.

B can move the hand to another place on the body if it feels called somewhere else. Repeat the inquiry, "What's here now?"

After several minutes, A withdraws the hand and places B's own hand in the same spot. Rest here for 1-2 minutes. A assists B to sit up and switch roles. Repeat.

Variations

You can ask for feedback in between rounds, or maintain sacred silence through the practice and transition and open for feedback at the end.

Attributions

Submitted by Rachel Santos of www.HeartOn.life and The Connection Movement.

**Unconditional Hugs

Setup
Full Group

Time
10-15 min

In Austin, this has become a favorite game, with some regular attendees calling it the deepest one they've experienced.

Instructions for Playing

Half the room stands in an outside circle facing in, the other half in an inside circle facing out.

Outside circle people close their eyes. Inside group people give random hugs to the people with closed eyes.

Best way to do consent.... If someone doesn't want to be hugged, they can still stand in the circle with eyes closed, but put their arms around themselves (signaling not to be hugged).

The game is best played silent, so that huggers are anonymous.

It's good to tap your partner on the arm or shoulder before hugging so they know to receive you and aren't caught by surprise.

Variations

We sometimes play this game with the outside circle as the huggers, inside circle receiving, and let people share in pairs and then to the full group at the end.

Notes

From Daniel Johnson of Authentic Relating Philadelphia.

**Angel Walk

This activity isn't really a game, and it comes from somewhere far before the Authentic Relating community. But it is damn powerful.

Instructions for Playing

Put on slow music and darken the room.

Have participants and facilitators mix and form 2 lines facing each other.

Have one person at a time close their eyes and move slowly down the line, while everyone on either side touches and guides them through the experience.

Optionally, participants can take a moment to whisper individual appreciations and love as others walk through the line (this may make the game a lot longer, so suggest with care).

At the end, each person is received and held by facilitators. It should take a few minutes for each person to pass through the line. After they pass through, they join the line at the end to support others.

Facilitator Instructions

This game should be played preferably after several hours or days of group activity, when the group feels open and safe with each other. We like doing it with live music played by someone in the community, and ending it with a group song that gets repeated several times.

Edge
Games

Edge Games

"Lean into your edge" is one of our favorite agreements for game nights, retreats, and trainings, because your edge is the space where your comfort zone meets your zone of expansion. This territory is often where you can grow the fastest and accomplish deep work that accelerates your abilities by leaps and bounds.

Edge games are not for entry-level participants. These games are a little more hardcore in terms of the level of vulnerability they require and the greater potential for expansion. Some of them require that players already know each other. Make sure to build up to these by creating psychological safety via deft facilitation.

Map of the Territory

· Fly on the Wall and Impression Spectrum are highly honest, powerful, and challenging feedback games that require experience with each other.

· Imitation Introduction and Body Love let others see and reflect us at a deep level, even if we are meeting for the first time.

· Great Guru Game asks/lets us to give up responsibility for our experience to someone else.

When to use Edge Games:

· At get-togethers between self-help junkies, edgy work retreats, and with open/experienced AR participants

· To bond an established group through sharing an intense experience

· At or near the end of a session

Index

· *Fly On The Wall
· Great Guru Game
· Impression Spectrum

· Imitation Introduction
· +Apology Process
· Body Love

**Fly On the Wall

Setup
Full Group

Time
25-40 min per fly

This is an extremely powerful way to give feedback, and should be balanced by a round of appreciation if done at a high level of spiciness.

Instructions for Playing

One person volunteers to be the fly, and chooses whether they want reflections to be "mild, medium, or spicy".

That person sits to the side of the group, facing away, and others have a conversation about them as if they are not present for 10-15 minutes.

Tailor the extravagance of your projections to the level of spiciness that the fly has requested. Even if you don't know the person you're gossiping about, you'd be surprised at how perceptive you are. Just say what you've noticed about them.

When time is up, have the fly rejoin the group to talk and/or recieve questions for 20 minutes about what did or didn't land, and what he/she felt with each reflection.

Variations

- Fly on the Cuddle Pile:
  Only speak positive noticings or judgments about the fly. You can use a derisive tone, as if you're really gossiping, but speak appreciations instead.

- Gecko on the Wall:
  For 2 minutes, a participant shares about a future they want to come true, in as much detail as possible. Then they turn their back to the group.
  For 3 minutes, the others "positively gossip" about that person's fantasy already having come true. i.e. "Have you guys seen Sara lately? I ran into her the other day while I was out shopping, and she looked radiant! I asked her what's been going on, and she told me all about her new career as a handler for exotic pets! She couldn't stop gushing about tortoises and giant spiders."
  The participant then turns back around. For 2 minutes, they describe the impact of hearing their fantasy come true.

Attributions

Developed by Authentic World. Fly on the Cuddle Pile variation by Laila Amerman, Gecko on the Wall variation by David Staab and Eli Slater.

Impression Spectrum

Setup
Full Group

Time
15-30 minutes

This is an edgy game, but also juicy, and is a great lead-in to withholds.

Instructions for Playing

One person volunteers to sit in the "hot seat", with the understanding that they will get a visual representation of people's subjective experience of them.

Name one end of the room the "I fucking love this person" corner or side and the other end of the room the "I really don't like how this person is showing up."

The person in the hot seat closes their eyes. And everyone moves to the point on the "spectrum" they experience that person as.

The person in the hot seat can open their eyes, take in where everyone is on the spectrum, and has the opportunity to ask up to three people why they are standing where they are. Those people can choose to give an explanation or pass.

Facilitator Instructions

At the start of each turn, ask everyone to reset to the middle of the space before they sort again. You can use other spectrum questions as well.

Attributions

Developed by Sara Katelyn Yeater (Sky) of Authentic Houston.

Imitation
Introduction

Setup
Full Group

Time
10-20 minutes

Created at the staff pre-meeting for an Authentic Leadership and Facilitation Training.
Most members knew each other, but a few were new to the group, and were able to pick up on the game anyways. It was enlivening, sweet, hilarious, and awkward, and formed a great start to bonding with the team.

This is listed as an edge game because many people find imitation a very vulnerable form of being seen.

Instructions for Playing

Form pairs in a circle, and choose an A and a B.

A takes 2 minutes to discover B's unique superpower - what they're really uniquely good at, and how that expresses in each moment. Switch roles.

Then, go around the circle. Each person introduces their partner as themselves, saying the name and superpower while embodying the other's way of being. For example, if my partner introduced me, he might sit very still, look deliberately around the circle, and say, "I'm Sara. I am a force for constructive chaos in the world. I create authenticity through my mere presence, and spark community wherever I go."

While saying this, he would imitate my body movements, speed and tone of speech, and other nonverbal cues. Optional applause after each introduction.

Attributions

Invented by Sara Ness

Body Love

Setup
Pairs

Time
15-20 min

We all have bodies. Yet for most of us, they as are much a source of shame as of joy. This game can be deeply healing for body shame, through the simple power of witnessing. I've really enjoyed playing this with romantic partners.

Instructions for Playing

Divide into pairs and pick an A and B.

Person A will be seen, person B will be the seer. Partners may sit or stand.

Person A begins by spending 3 minutes appreciating 3 of their own body parts, such as:
"I like my stomach because I used to hold a lot of tension there, but I started putting more care into my breathing and now it feels more relaxed. Also, I can now look in the mirror without judging it as much. I think its curves are beautiful."

Person A may then take a minute to define any boundaries they may have, such as:
"Don't speak about my stomach, arms, or breasts."
"You can talk about anything, but I may ask you to stop if I start feeling uncomfortable around an area."

Person B then spends 3-5 minutes appreciating 3 body parts of person A. These may be the same or different as person A originally mentioned. Go slowly with this, and check in periodically to see if A is full up or okay to hear more.

Afterwards, person A takes one minute to share impact and show a sign of appreciation.

Switch roles and repeat.

Great Guru Game

Setup
Triads

Time
1-2 hours

To play this game, triads need to have a shared history of relationship and experience over time, like a multi-month course. They should know each other's ins-and-outs fairly well, and have a good sense of each other's essence & shadow. If this is not the case, this exercise will not yield the intended results. This is not an early-stage relating game.

Instructions for Playing

Divide into triads of people that know each other.

Participant A acts as Guru first. B sits below A, and starts by naming an appreciation or superpower they perceive (or imagine) in the other. "Oh Great Guru! Your gift is..."

Then B asks a question of Guru A, ideally something they're struggling with in their own life, as they would ask of a guru they had traveled many miles and weeks to see. A answers from their highest wisdom. This whole section should take about 3 minutes.

After answering, Guru A gives B a devotional practice that can be done right then and there, potentially involving C or other triads in the room, to help them explore and express their question. A does this by saying: "What I want from you to express your wholeness more fully is...And to express this, my practice for you is..." They have 2 minutes to describe this.

B can only object to the practice if they believe it will cause significant and/or irrevocable harm to themselves or others. Otherwise, they must try it for 2 minutes, while Guru A and partner C repeatedly say "YES!!" or "MORE!!"

After A completes the practice, Guru A shares wisdom and direction again: "What I LOVED about that was..." and "What I would need more of is..." for 1-2 minutes.

A does the practice again for 2-3 minutes, taking in this feedback, with the others cheering them on. They complete their turn with silent appreciation, applause, and/or a breath.

Partner C may now work with Guru A (for a longer version of the game where everyone gets to be Guru twice), or switch so that C is Guru and B is the petitioner.

Notes

From Michael Porcelli, invented for the ARC training.

+Apology Process

Setup
Pairs

Time
30 min

This game explores acknowledging and practicing giving an apology, with the added twist of not getting too much into the details of the story behind the situation.

Instructions for Playing

In pairs, choose a person A and B. Person A is the "Apologist", and person B is the "Listener". Person A closes their eyes and connects with a meaningful apology they have not given, or can not give. Take a few breaths. Facilitator gives the following directions:

A word on stories and secrets: When I am in a place I consider safe, a closed container with people who I connect with, I feel open to sharing much more than I would otherwise. This can later lead to a "vulnerability hangover". But if I stay present with my feelings, reactions, and perceptions in the moment, then I can remain fully authentic without revealing details that I may later regret having shared.

 In this spirit, I invite you to talk without getting too much into story. For example, instead of saying "Bob, I acknowledge that I broke your arm and then laughed and didn't believe you when you said you were in pain," I would say "I acknowledge that I hurt and laughed at you."

This is an invitation: it is not wrong to share details, but do remember to Honor Self and others if you choose to do so.

Using the following reflection prompts, person A uses the sentence stems in their apology process while person B listens.

Acknowledgement
"I acknowledge that I hurt you when I...."   (Acknowledging the hurt)
"I understand that the hurt you experienced was..."   (Understanding the hurt)
"When you held me accountable, I felt..."
"When others held me accountable, I felt..."
"When I was defensive about this, it felt like..." (What is it like to feel defensive? When might it be helpful? When not?)

Impact and understanding
"When I realized what I had done, I felt..." (What's it like to realize I've hurt someone?)

"When I saw the impact on you, I felt..." (What's it like to see someone's pain and know I'm the/a cause?)

<u>Amends</u>
"If you would like, I could make amends by..." (Doesn't have to be proportional.)
"I plan to avoid hurting someone this way again by..."

Then, person B the Listener: ask the Apologist how they want you to respond. To the best of your ability (while honoring self), respond that way.

Afterward, B share your experience with A, "I felt you the most when...".

<u>Large Group Share</u>
 "What was it like apologizing? What was it like listening? Asking for the listener to respond in a certain way? Being asked to respond in a certain way? Responding?

Facilitator Instructions

Do this process in break out pairs. Read out the sentence stems to the whole group while the pairs are looking at each other. Provide a way for the pairs to use the sentence stems together.

Attributions

David Betz-Zall

Transpersonal Games

Transpersonal Games

Have you ever experienced a moment when the boundaries between yourself and others fell away? Where you felt like you were not only sharing the same reality, but experiencing it in the same way?

Transpersonal Games can help us achieve this sense of oneness. From eye contact to simultaneous reflection, projecting ourselves into others' shoes to hearing our words from others' mouths, these games instigate a connection that goes far beyond the physical.

Map of the Territory

· Prolonged Eye Contact, ...AND..., and Color Echo use nonverbal or nonsense contact to effect a hypnotizing state of connection.

· Watermelon, Translator, and Terminator are projection games that playfully shove us into channeling others' realities.

· Whispered Belongings weaves an appreciative experience with a whole group.

When to use Transpersonal Games:

· Near the end of retreats and other sessions
· As a warmup for embodiment and touch games, or for circling
· In conferences or events focused around the "we-space"

Index

Prolonged Eye Contact

Setup
Pairs

Time
5-15 min

This game is intense for many people, as we don't often spend much time in direct eye contact with each other. Historically, prolonged eye contact signaled aggression. Now, it can be a form of deep connection and shared meditation that leads to a breakdown in the distinction between self and other.

Instructions for Playing

Have two circles of chairs, one facing out and one facing in. Participants sit across from each other and make eye contact without speaking for between 30 seconds and 5 minutes. Then take group sharebacks.

Facilitator Instructions

I would suggest keeping the time frame for eye contact short to start with, unless you are working with a community already comfortable with this sort of connection or want to push people.

Variations

- Guided Eye Contact: Every minute, while participants are in eye contact, give instructions such as: "show vulnerability to the other person", "show compassion," "look at the other person as you think they would like to be looked at", etc.

Attributions

Eyegazing practices are as old as looking into each others' eyes.

...AND...

This game explores how it is to be connected and separate from each other as human beings. It's trippy.

Instructions for Playing

This is a nonverbal meditation. In pairs come to silence facing each other.

First focus on your connectedness to each other - that you are sharing the same world with each other, that you can on some level relate to each other's emotion, each other's life and experiences. Deeper yet, that your partner could be a mirror for yourself.

Take a minute or two to share with each other what it's like to be ONE.

Then focus on how the other is a strange being, a universe unto itself, never fully knowable even to itself.

Take a minute or two to share with each other what it's like to be TWO.

Then, read this Rumi quote:
"You think because you understand 'one' you must also understand 'two', because one and one make two. But you must also understand 'and'." Focus on the 'and'".

Prompt participants to consider: What is it like being one, and two? Being alone, and together? Knowing and not knowing?

Thank each other for the interaction. Then take group shares.

Facilitator Instructions

Guide the participants into the meditation with the prompts, expanding on them and taking pauses after each contemplation to let them connect with the ideas while looking in each other's eyes. I sometimes play this as a mingling game, where walk around before finding a partner.

Attributions

Invented by Sara Ness of the Austin Love Juggernaut.

Color Echo

Setup
Pairs

Time
5-15 min

This game seems simple, but it has kicked me into deep moments of shared reality.

Instructions for Playing

Divide into pairs.

One person in each pair begins saying items in a category that you pick, such as colors, numbers, or emotions. The other person in the pair echoes the word back, in any way they desire. Then switch.

Finally, either person can initiate the word. Take shares at the end.

Variations

- Telepathy: The other person should try to say the same word at the same time (bonus: with the same cadence!).

- Mirroring: Play with body movement, one partner leading and the other "mirroring". Try two rounds, starting with movement alone, then adding vocal categories (or just primal vocal sounds).

- Combo: One partner leads movement, the other leads vocal!

- "I Know What You're Thinking About...": Stop the game halfway through and instruct participants to "Make it sexier". Resume and watch the heat rise . . .

Attributions

Invented by Decker Cunov of Authentic World.
Variations from Ross Cooper of Authentic Houston.

**Watermelon

Setup
Pairs

Time
10 min

"Watermelon" helps participants realize how much nonverbal communication informs their understanding of another's state, and can lead to profound moments of shared reality.

Instructions for Playing

Get into pairs and decide on an A and a B. During the game, A's should only say the word "Watermelon". B's should respond with, "You seem . . ." A's "Watermelon" should be an authentic response to what they feel after B's evaluation. B's read into what they think their partner is experiencing, and project into that with the "You seem..."

Continue back and forth like this for 3-5 minutes. Pair sharebacks and full-group.

For a fun variation, try having Bs and As both complete the sentence stem, "What I really get about you is . . ." at the end of the game.

Variations

- "Hi, My Name Is...": Instead of saying "Watermelon", let people introduce themselves: "Hi, my name is..." followed by "You seem..."

Attributions

From Authentic World Variation by Ross Cooper of Authentic Houston

**Translator

Setup
Quads

Time
10-15 min

We play this game at almost every advanced retreat now, often with groups of 16 or more people (8 speakers, 8 translators) having a conversation about anything and switching roles every 15-20 minutes. The game continues until it hits a depth where the format no longer makes sense, by which point the group is deeply bonded (or highly triggered, which is also valuable to work through!) and we switch into circling.

Instructions for Playing

Each member is assigned a number- 1, 2, 3, and 4.

· #1 completes a sentence stem, or begins a conversation, possibly in response to a prompt the facilitator gives. Ex. "What I notice about you is that your shirt is tight."
· #2 translates this into unfiltered language, saying what they think is really behind their partner's words, ex. "You're hot and I want to hit on you, but not be too direct about it."
· #3 responds, ex. "I feel uncomfortable hearing that."
· #4 translates, ex. "I don't want to be in this situation now."

Back to #1's turn, and 1 and 3 keep going for 3-20 minutes (or until the game feels complete) with their translators speaking what's "really" going on. Then swap roles.

Facilitator Instructions

This game can be played two ways - either give everyone two simple sentence stem options at the beginning and let them choose which one they use at any point, or introduce a topic to speak about. After a while, each group will find its own distinct dynamic and the prompt won't matter anymore.

In-the-moment speakers (#1 and #3) can respond to each other or to the translation, whatever feels most alive and keeps the game going. Speakers shouldn't correct their translators unless truly uncomfortable, in which case they can pause the game to clarify.

For the first few rounds of speaking, you'll have to pause participants who begin responding before the last person's translator speaks. Eventually the group will start monitoring itself.

Attributions

This game was developed by Annabeth Novitski of the Austin Love Juggernaut, with variations by many later players. It's based on the "Obama's Anger Translator" sketch by Key and Peele.

Terminator

This is similar to the Translator and Watermelon games. If participants take it seriously, it can be both profound and hilarious, creating deep moments of unexpected understanding and insight.

Instructions for Playing

Form pairs, then quads. In each quad, one pair will be asking questions and the other will be answering. Choose an A and a B in the answering pair.

Here's the twist: the question-askers can only pose their questions using the pronoun "we" (as in, "we're curious about..." or "we imagine you're..."), regardless of whether they think it's also their partner's experience. Also, although B is the one being asked questions, A is answering for them, playing the role of "Spirit Face".

Example:
Questioner 1 - "We notice that you scratch your head whenever you're asked about your family. What's happening for you in that moment?" B (being asked the question): stays silent. A, intuiting: "I'm trying to think of a way to answer that won't paint my family in a bad light, even though I have mixed feelings about my childhood."

In-the-moment or personal-experience questions are best, such as "what's this like for you?", similar to what's used in circling. Stay away from the informational, unless you want this to become an improv game - A should be trying to intuit B's answers, not make them up.

Play for 5-7 minutes. Then debrief, switch roles, and repeat for as many rounds as you want. If everyone plays every role, the game will take about 30 minutes, plus direction time.

Attributions

Invented by Mike Blas for an Austin circling lab.

Whispered Belongings

Setup
Pairs

Time
20 minutes

Materials
Paper and pens

Instructions for Playing

Get into pairs and have paper and pens ready.

Everyone gets comfortable, and imagine something you wish would be said to you to make you feel loved, connected and belong. Take 3 minutes for this.

After everyone has a statement, write it down and set it out to show to the other person.

Both in the pair read the other's statement silently, and do not speak, but make eye contact if able after reading it. After a minute of this the person in the pair with the lightest eyes stands. The other in the pair remains sitting.

The sitters may keep their eyes open or shut depending on how edgy they would like this, and also should keep out their statement so others can read it.

The people standing are then informed to walk around to who they are drawn to and whisper that person's statement in their ear, or just use eye contact to connect. This will happen for about 4-5 minutes.

Standers sit and switch roles. After another 3-4 minutes of the same the pairs come back together.

Each person is given 2 minutes to share any follow up of what came up for them during this exercise. It's powerful to have a group share after this too.

Facilitator Instructions

Provide the paper and pens for all the participants and keep time. You can ring a bell to prompt the switches.

Attributions

Invented by Kim Marie Glynn.

Resourcing Games

Resourcing Games

Marshall Rosenberg, the founder of Nonviolent Communication, wrote that, "Every criticism, judgment, diagnosis, and expression of anger is the tragic expression of an unmet need."

But how do we meet our needs? It takes self-reflection to even know what we need. It takes courage to make a clear request that might help us meet that need. And if we are the person receiving the request, it can take practice to tune into our bodies and decline a request that isn't a whole body yes.

Resourcing games create practice space for participants to understand their needs, make requests, set boundaries, and own their authentic desires. No filter!

Map of the Territory

· Minis creates a simple space for another to support us through presence.

· Asking for Support, The Giving Game, and The Receiving Game let us request what we need from others, with the option for them to provide it.

· Bacon and Advice are creative formats for others to intuit and give what we need.

· Mirror Mirror, Higher Self-Talk, and Love and Self-Love challenge us to give resource, insight, and appreciation to ourselves.

When to use Resourcing Games:

· Usually in the middle to end of a session, though Minis is good in the beginning

· In trainings on boundaries, consent, desire, touch and/or people-pleasing

· To give participants a chance to help and heal each other

Index

Minis

Setup
Pairs

Time
7 minutes

This is a beautiful, quick game to establish presence and help participants arrive into themselves and into the group.

Instructions for Playing

In pairs, decide who is A and who is B.

B has 3 minutes to do, say, or express whatever they want in order to become more present in the moment.

A witnesses B without speaking or engaging.

When 3 minutes is up, A asks a presencing question, like "What color are your socks right now?" or "How does your left finger feel?" Switch and repeat.

Variations

- A variation of this game is to let A assist B in becoming more present, by moving with them or responding to requests B makes.

Attributions

Experienced during a Luminous Body workshop in Boulder.
The presencing questions have obvious roots in Co-Counseling.

Asking for Support

Setup
Pairs

Time
15-20 minutes

At the core of many of our struggles is an unmet need. This game can help develop the skill to turn our unmet needs into a request so we can try to get the support we need to feel complete again, while staying in relationship with others.

Instructions for Playing

Pair up and take a few seconds to make silent eye contact and get present with each other.

Person A has 2 minutes to share with B using this sentence stem: "What I'm currently struggling with...."

Then, ask A to participate in a 1 minute guided meditation:

"Close your eyes and feel into your struggle. Try to stay with the core feeling you are struggling with inside. Can you feel an unmet need underneath? Maybe a need for significance, love or certainty? Is there anything the other person could do to help address your need? Try to imagine a concrete request you could make. Now try to have compassion for your struggle: "May I be able to let go of my anger, fears and worries? May I find a deeper peace of mind?"

Person A opens their eyes and has 1 min to make a request to B using this sentence stem: "I'm feeling ... would you have a moment to support me?" If yes, then proceed with "What would really support me is...." B has 2 minutes to try to provide A with the support they asked for.

Switch roles and debrief after both pairs have gone.

Attributions

Asking for Support comes from Patrick Wolf in LA.

**The Giving Game (Would You?)

The intent of this game is to tune into desire, whether or not you receive what you're wanting. That includes recognizing the desire to NOT fulfill a given request. It also includes being aware of what you want, even if you think it isn't something you can get. I love playing this on dates!

Instructions for Playing

In pairs, choose an A and a B. A has a few minutes (5-10 works well) to ask for exactly what they want from, or with B in the moment. Requests can be physical, mental, or emotional ("Would you tell me what you think about me? Would you give me a back rub? Would you tell me about your childhood?").

B's have the option to either fulfill the request, say no, or make a counter-offer.

A's keep making requests until their time is up, and should be encouraged to keep asking for specifics until they get exactly what they want, provided B wants to give it ("Would you rub my back AND tell me what you find attractive about me, whispered into my ear, while I'm leaning against you? And now could you rub a little harder and further up my spine? And speak in a deeper voice? And now would you tell me how you feel about all the requests I'm making?").

Switch roles. Sharebacks.

Facilitator Instructions

Prompt As to check in with themselves and their intention before making requests, to ask for what they really want, and to use specifics until fully satisfied. Prompt Bs to say no if they feel hesitation to agree, and to recognize and respect their own boundaries.

Variations

- Tuning into Desire: Before playing, participants partner up and give A's a space to ask for what they most want from/with B for 1-2 minutes, with B's just listening and not giving or responding at all. Share impact, switch, and optionally rotate partners a few times before taking the option of action.

- Hot Giving Game: Form two circles of participants, the outer circle facing in and the inner circle facing out. Pairs have 10 seconds of eye contact to get present with each other, and then 30 seconds to complete the stem, "What I'm wanting from this exchange is..." Each partner has 2-3 minutes to play the Giving Game (above). Pairs give sharebacks, then the outer circle moves over one to rotate partners.

- Alien Consent Game: Participants take turns "asking" in alien gibberish. Partners feel for their yes or no and give an answer. If yes, groups act out and improvise what they just "agreed" to.

Attributions

Adapted from the Authentic Woman Experience, with variations by the Austin Love Juggernaut. It has become one of our favorites.

The Receiving Game
(Would I?)

Setup
Triads

Time
15-20 minutes

This game is a hybrid of Would You? and Agency and Communion. It was inspired by the theme of Agency and having permission to exercise choice in a compassionate container. It intentionally didn't invite collaborating or choosing both offers out of a desire to see what participants would do with these "tools of agency." This one seems like a ripe game for Honor-Self rule breakers...

Instructions for Playing

Choose an A, B, and C. A's will be the "Deliberator" in each round. Both B and C make requests to A, who then deliberates out loud and chooses one winning request. Because of the nature of this game and who your A might be, the request doesn't need to be practical or "doable" in the allotted time.

First, slow down with a guided meditation where B's and C's drop into themselves and what they REALLY want from A.

B's then make their request and have A reveal how they are initially receiving that request, somatically and/ or emotionally. This takes approximately 1.5 minutes.
If it seems necessary, take a moment for A to drop back into themselves to receive the next request.

It is now C's turn to make the request and for A to reveal how they are initially receiving that request, somatically and/or emotionally. A's then have 2 minutes to verbally weigh the two requests and choose (with the option to counter-offer). Repeat this process with each member of the triad.

Attributions

Created by Sara Katelyn Yeater (Sky) of Authentic Houston.

**Bacon

This game was created with the intent of feeding the leaders of the community so that they can feed the community. Wouter (the game developer) regularly plays it the day after weekend workshops for inner crew members.

Instructions for Playing

Group splits into 3 roles: Angels, Recipients, and Free agents.

Ask, "If there was an essential nutrient deficient, keeping the Recipient from reaching their whole brilliance, what would it be?"

Angels take ±10 minutes to get clear on what is missing in the Recipients' life right now (using authentic relating skills), then take ±20 minutes to make it happen, drawing in Free agents as needed.

Switch roles until everyone has gotten a chance to give, clarify, and receive.

Attributions

Developed by Wouter Slegers of Authentic Europe.

Advice

Setup
Pairs

Time
10 min

This game's purpose is to show that advice can be a legitimate way to care for another, but it's much more helpful if we know we are about to receive advice and actually want it.

Instructions for Playing

Divide the room into pairs.

Partner A takes 2 minutes to talk about a situation in their life where they want something to be different, or they just aren't satisfied with things the way they are now.

Partner B asks: "Do you want advice?"
If A says yes - > give advice for 1 min.
If A says no - > offer a shoulder rub or a hug, or anything that would feel caring to partner B (check in before acting on the offer) for 1 min.

Attributions

From Jason Digges of the Integral Center

Mirror, Mirror

Setup
Pairs

Time
15-20 min

Often, it can be easier to give advice to others than to ourselves. This game lets us do both!

Instructions for Playing

Separate into pairs, A and B, and have each person think of a situation they would ask others for advice, wish to change, or simply wish to gain perspective.

A then spends 2-3 minutes describing the situation to their partner.

B repeats verbatim what A said for 1-2 minutes, without changing the pronouns and with as much the same emotion/inflection as remaining authentic allows so that it is as though the situation is happening to themselves.

B concludes by asking A, "Do you have any advice for me?"

A then answers the request for advice for 2-3 minutes.

Repeat the process, changing roles.

Attributions

Emma Joe Anderson of Authentic Houston.

Higher Self-Talk

Setup
Breakout Groups

Time
30-45 min

This game is something like a self-focused Guru Game, and an awesome practice of self-discovery.

Instructions for Playing

Get into small groups (4-6 people).

One person in each group stands behind their chair and embodies their higher self.

The others ask questions of the higher self. For example, if Rob is playing the game, his group could ask Rob's higher self, "How do you feel about Rob?" "Does Rob listen to you?" "What do you want to tell Rob?" or, more generally, "What is your purpose in life?" "How do you feel?" etc.

Spend 5-7 minutes with each person.

Attributions

Developed by Jordan Myska Allen for Integral Austin.

**Love and Self-Love

Setup
Triads

Time
1 hour

This game is a perfect mixture of group connection and personal depth. It's also interesting for exploring our comfort with loving ourselves vs loving others. This sticks with me as one of my absolute favorite games, if only for how full of love I feel after playing it.

Instructions for Playing

Choose who will go first (A).

A tells the others in their group about somebody they love for 3-5 minutes, really getting in touch with that love and care as they tell it.

Take 3-4 minutes for the other group members (B and C) to say how the share impacted them (what they felt, what they get about that person's connection, etc.).

Next, A talks for 3-5 min about why they love themselves, with as much care and feeling as used in talking about the other.

Other group members share impact for 3-4 min.

Facilitator Instructions

Shuffle the groups (or keep them together) and switch who is sharing.

Attributions

Decker Cunov led this game at an Alethia in Boulder in July 2013

181

Appreciation Games

Appreciation Games

Who doesn't enjoy having their love tank filled up? A little bit of structure can give us a reliable opportunity to make someone else's day, week, or month.

Appreciation games allow participants to give each other the gift of being seen for being themselves. These games create moments of inspiration, acknowledgement, gratitude and love. They are great before and after edgy/intense games or experiences.

Map of the Territory

· Gratitude Journal and Magical Moments prompt us to reflect on experiences we feel grateful for in our own lives.

· Love Blaster and Sketch Appreciation let us appreciate through the simple act of noticing what's here, and seeing it with new eyes.

· Like Like Goose, Appreciation Dyads, and Appreciation Hot Seat require improvisation about what we appreciation, and can be played even with strangers.

· Shower of Love, Ending Appreciations, Community Appreciations, and Intimacies are great ending games for any event, allowing each person a chance to receive.

When to use Appreciation Games:

· Gratitude games work well to open up the heart early in sessions
· Before and/or after heavier feedback games and shadowy games
· When you want to heap love onto a special person like a birthday celebrant
· At the end of a retreat or training to leave people on a love high

Index

· Gratitude Journal
· Appreciation Days
· Magical Moments
· *Shower of Love
· *Love Blaster

· Ending Appreciations
· *Sketch Appreciations
· Community Appreciations
· Like, Like, GOOSE!
· *Intimicies

Gratitude
Journal

Setup
Breakout
Groups

Time
15 min

Materials
Paper and pens

"I took this from the field of positive psychology, mostly Tal Ben-Shahar's Harvard lecture series (available on YouTube and highly recommended). The standard gratitude journal is to write 5 things down in a journal at the end of every day and meditate with them in your heart for 10 minutes, and really be thankful for what you have in your life."
- Chris

Instructions for Playing

Played in groups of 3-5 people. Each person gets a slip of paper and something to write with.

Take a few minutes to write down 3 things that you are really truly grateful for. As with anything in Authenticity, really sit and reflect on what you are grateful for right now in life, and not write something down just to play the game. Make it meaningful.

In groups, each participant gets a period of time (recommend 75 seconds per subject) to express to the rest of the group why the items you wrote down are meaningful to you.

Facilitator Instructions

I recommend using a bell to move between items and rounds to keep the momentum moving; not giving one topic enough time or too much time can really impact its felt importance to the listener and speaker. I set it up right after "Complain Game" and "Higher Self-Talk." This way people go from complaining, to the voice of their higher self, to being grateful for what they have in their lives. People took notice and really liked it.

Attributions

This game comes from Chris Gongaware of Feel the Real Oahu.

Magical Moments

Setup
Full Group or
Breakout Groups

Time
15-25 minutes

This exercise is a guided excursion down a magical path on memory lane.

Instructions for Playing

Everyone takes a moment to center themselves in a meditation, optionally using the following text:

Let's take a moment to center ourselves. Take a deep breath in as you count to 8 (count to 8), and exhale as you count to 8 (count to 8) as you release all conscious thoughts from your mind. Slowly close your eyes. Think of a moment in your life that felt magical to you. Whatever comes to mind first. Remember everything you can about all the nuances of that experience. What did you smell during that moment? Which colors did you see? What sounds did you hear? How loud or soft were the sounds? Was there music? What did things feel like to the touch? What textures did you experience against which parts of your body? What did you taste, if anything? What mood do you remember being in? Bring your awareness to that moment. Relive it, now.

Then think of a moment in life that felt magical, going into detail recalling the memory with all your senses. Take a minute or so to relive that magical experience. It's common to hear chuckles and other expressions.

Then slowly open your eyes, and go around the circle to share experiences with the sentence stem "A magical moment I remember is..." Include as many colors, smells, tastes, textures, moods to the story as you can, to paint a palpable experience for all listeners.

Attributions

Created by Roxanne Jarrett.

**Love Blaster

Setup
Singles, then pairs,
then quads

Time
15 min

Love Blaster is an instant wonderment-and-joy-inducer, and a way to notice choice in your frame of awareness. It's also fun to experience a different take on gossip - talking about what you appreciate about each other to each other!

Instructions for Playing

Each participant chooses an object in the room. For 1-2 minutes, notice and appreciate everything about it, verbally or nonverbally. Then close your eyes, to notice and appreciate the feeling of appreciation.

Then in partners, choose another object, and appreciate it together for 2-3 minutes, talking about what you see and enjoy.

Finally, each pair (A and B) finds another pair (C and D). For 2 minutes, A and B can whisper to each other about things they notice and appreciate about C and D, without letting C and D hear (or, for extra intensity, do this by turns so that the other pair can hear!). C and D do the same. Then take 2-3 minutes for the pairs to share their appreciations with each other.

End with a short meditation for participants to appreciate the feeling of appreciation within oneself. Sharebacks!

Facilitator Instructions

This would be an interesting game to pair with games around judgment, of self and/or of others, and with a longer meditation inviting participants to notice and appreciate each sensation inside their bodies

Variations

· Extra Squish: For use if you want the game to go a few minutes longer, or don't have exact quads. After appreciating an object in pairs, the pairs make eye contact with each other in silence. Experiencing the same quality of attention and appreciation for the person across from them... enjoying that person's physical features, savoring the way that person just appreciated the object, reveling in any shared history. Then, notice that the same quality of appreciation is being given to them - that somebody thinks them worthy of just as much wonderment and joy as they've been giving out. Watch the smiles...then move into quads, or end the game with sharebacks.

· Appreciation Trinity: Played in pairs, then quads, then pairs, with one person in each pair bringing their phone (on airplane mode) or a mirror for later use. First, each pair chooses an object in the room and spends 7-10 minutes noticing and appreciating everything about it verbally with each other, as they might in an art museum. Next pairs then join into quads. Each original pair whispers noticings and appreciations of the other pair, as if gossiping. Then allow 3-5 minutes for the quads to share these appreciations aloud among themselves. Lastly, the original pairs bring out their phone or mirror and use it to view themselves. Partner A begins appreciating themself as partner B witnesses. When A might get stuck, B can provide a prompt or suggest ideas such as "What do you like about your eyes?" After 4-5 minutes, partners switch roles. Leave time for processing and debriefing.

Attributions

Sara Ness developed this for Thanksgiving Games in Austin, Variations by Amy Silverman.

**Sketch Appreciation

Setup
Pairs

Time
15-30 min

This game can be especially intimate and playing with your beloved brings it to another level.

"The first time this was played was at the 2016 All-Texas AR Retreat at Camp Young-Judea. We played late at night around the campfire, which provided a glow and shadow across the faces that was magical. We spent over 30 minutes in sharebacks and every participant had a powerful piece to share. The second time was played at the Authentimacy Partner Playshop facilitated by Brave and I in Austin." ~Megan

Instructions for Playing

Participants divide into pairs, sitting across from each other. Take a minute or two for eye-gazing.

Choose a person A and person B. A begins to appreciate B. Now A pretends they are an artist and B is their masterpiece. Imagine you have all the tools available to you for this masterpiece: watercolor, clay, charcoal, crayon, whatever you decide.

Now take your tool, and begin to sketch your partner. Check your assumption with touch, and lean into the edge of placing your finger lightly over their skin to touch as you begin to sketch them into life, tracing their features, wrinkles, freckles. Watch their expression change and retrace if desired.

Take a deep breath at the end and take 30 seconds for silent noticing.

Follow-up with 5-7 minutes of sharebacks from both A and B. Switch and repeat with B sketching A.

Facilitator Instructions

Read paragraph 2 and 3 as guiding instructions to the participants.

Attributions

Created by Brave Legend Pietri and Megan Rose Browning of the Austin Love Juggernaut and Alchemy of We.

Like, Like, GOOSE!

Setup
Full group

Time
20-30 min

A twist on a classic childrens' game. Played like the original, only the "ducks" are substituted for things the speaker likes about the person they're touching.

While it can be hard for participants to come up with answers quickly, especially in groups that know each other well, this can be a fun way to bring some movement and spontaneity into group truth. The judgment variation is an edgy exercise that elicits the emotional impact of being judged or judging in a playful, elementary fashion.

Instructions for Playing

One person walks around the outside of the circle lightly touching the head of participants as they pass, stating a one-word appreciation about each of them.

When ready, the appreciator can instead say "GOOSE!" and that participant must chase the appreciator around the circle before they reach the empty chair.

If they succeed in tagging, that person remains in their role. If not, the goose becomes the appreciator. Play until your heart's content. Take 10 minutes for sharebacks.

Facilitator Instructions

Remind participants to respect themselves. The meat of this game lies in the sharebacks. How do we receive judgments? When judging, do we tend toward appreciation? Projection? Negativity? How does maturity play a role in giving and receiving judgment? While this game is rich with potential, it may warrant a follow-up game for love and appreciation such as "Love Blaster".

Variations

- Things I Like: The person tagging heads names things they have an affiliation for, like "basketball" or "meditation". When ready to choose a goose, they say something they DON'T resonate with (like "discussing politics"), tag, and run!

- Judgment, Judgment, GOOSE!: The "ducks" are substituted with an impulsive judgment made about the person receiving the pat on the head.

Notes

Originally invented by Megan Rose Browning of the Austin Love Juggernaut and Alchemy of We.

Appreciation Dyads

This is easily my favorite game to run at the end of a night.

Instructions for Playing

Pair up, decide on an A and a B.

Each person has 5 minutes to complete the stem: "Being with you, I appreciate..." (something in the present moment, either about themself, about the other person, or about both). Switch.

Optional: do this as a back-and-forth Noticing Appreciation Game.

Facilitator Instructions

Participants tend to run dry after the first couple of minutes, and the digging to find NEW things to appreciate leads to beautiful connection.

You can also switch partners between rounds (gauntlet-style)

Attributions

From Ross Cooper of Authentic Houston

+Appreciation
Hot Seat

Setup
Small groups (4-7 people), Full group

Time
5-10 min/person

Do we know each other well enough to complement each other in ways that land?
This can be super edgy for those who have trouble receiving appreciation.

Instructions for Playing

1 person volunteers to be in the Hot Seat.

Everyone else shares appreciations for them. These might be things we have experienced in this person, or they might be things we intuit are true of them.

The person in the Hot Seat will occasionally share their Rating 1-5 on how HOT it makes them to hear these.

Attributions

Submitted by David Betz-Zall and Laureli Shimayo Authentic Seattle

**Shower of Love

This game is quick, beautiful, just incredibly sweet.
I use it at the end of trainings, meetings, at birthday parties,
and whenever I want to make somebody blush.

Instructions for Playing

Each person gets a chance to be the focus of appreciation.

When the time starts, group members say out a word or two, whatever comes to mind, for that person - perhaps an essential quality they embody, an impact they have, an attribute that is appreciated.

Anybody can say words. Participants can also repeat a word somebody else has given that they agree with for that person. Let the words form an overlapping collage of acknowledgement for 1-2 minutes, setting a timer, then say "Thank you" to end the interaction when the timer goes off.

Move to the next person.

Ending
Appreciations

Setup
Full Group

Time
10-20 min

A sweet ending to any group event. If you have larger groups, make sure you leave extra time for everyone to go.

Instructions for Playing

Each person tells the person to their left (or right) something they appreciate about that person, focusing on interactions and impressions formed during the last few hours or day.

Attributions

I experienced this at Jordan Myska Allen's Integral meetup.

Community Appreciations

This is a lovely way to honor different sections of a community. It's a great game to end any weekend retreat or training.

Instructions for Playing

Form a standing circle.

Identify a sub-group of your community, such as "Facilitators," "Men," "Women," "People who attend every damn event," etc. That group of people stands up and moves into the center.

Then, ask for 3-5 people to appreciate either
a) a member of the selected group, or
b) the group as a whole, for something they have brought and the impact it had.

Attributions

Seen first at the Integral Center

**Intimacies

Setup
Full group

Time
10-20 min

This is the best game I know of to encourage 1:1 sharing of impact at the end of an event (or at any time in a community) with both privacy, choice, and a minimum of chaos. It works best with 16 or more participants, and thus is ideal for large retreats or conferences.

Instructions for Playing

Form an inner and an outer circle, with participants facing each other. Each should have a partner. Make sure there is enough space in the middle for people to move around.

Inner circle (A) will share an Intimacy with their partner on the outer circle (B). This can be a Truth, Withhold, or Appreciation ("When you [did this thing]...I felt..."), a Tag ("Something I'd like to follow up with you on is..."), a Projection they want to check ("A story I have about you is...is that true?"), or anything else they want to share from a space of developing or completing relationship.

When A has finished sharing, B "Thank you" and/or give a response based on A's share. They should NOT share a Truth, Withhold, Appreciation, Tag, or Projection in return - instead, they should fully receive and honor what they heard. Then, A and B switch places, so A is on the outer circle now.

B goes to find a new partner (anyone on the outer circle who is open), while A stands and waits for someone to come share with them.

Facilitator Instructions

Towards the end of this game, the structure often breaks down - people on the inner circle will start sharing with each other, and those on the outer will go find others to meet. I usually let this go, since it's a sign that connection has been accomplished.

This is a good game for the facilitator to participate in as well as lead. You'll get a lot of energy back from what you've given, and it's humanizing for people to see you take part.

You can also play this game in a circle of sitting participants, where anyone can get up, share with someone, and then take the chair of that person.

Attributions

Invented by Sara Ness of Authentic Revolution

Leadership
Games

Leadership Games

Many of us have a tricky relationship with power. We may want it, fear it, or run from it. Yet, trying to take power out of a group just means that the loudest or least developed people end up owning the most of it.

Leadership games create a fun space to feel what it's like to have power over another person or a group. How does your body feel when you are telling others what to do? Do you contract or expand when your words are elevated to guru-esque status? How do others feel in the presence of your leadership? We explore questions like these, so that we can hold power well in the times when it is ours to use.

Map of the Territory

- Far Away So Close, Kingdom, The Leader Game, and Guru Game put participants into the role of authority to explore what they do and why.

- Agency and Communion explores decision-making in groups.

- Block Ops allows participants to create and facilitate the experiences they fear most.

When to use Leadership Games:

- Mid to late in your session

- In leadership and facilitation trainings

- With groups or participants that seem uncomfortable with the concept, use, or function of power

- When exploring power dynamics in groups

Index

Far Away, So Close

Setup
Pairs

Time
10 min

This is a game that plays with both movement and power. If participants stick to the rules, it can be uncomfortable and profound; if allowed variance, it can be fun.

Instructions for Playing

Line up in two lines facing each other, at opposite ends of the room. One line is "A" and one is "B".

The "A"s will be directing the "B"s. Giving three hand signals: "Come Closer" (beckon), "Go Back" (reverse beckon), or "Stop" (hand up). Each person has 1-2 minutes to follow or direct, nonverbally.

Partners share their experience with each other, switch, play again, and group shareback.

Facilitator Instructions

There are two ways to instruct this game:

- Introduce only 3 hand signals: Go back, come closer, stop. Don't specify more, but don't stop participants from adding their own twists. They will often do so organically if not given instructions to stick only to the three signals.

- Allow only 3 hand signals: Go back, come closer, stop. Tell participants they can only use these signals, and to focus on what it feels like to direct, follow, be closer or further away, explore comfort zones.

Attributions

This game comes from Authentic World.

Kingdom

Setup
Full Group or
Breakout Groups

Time
15-20 min

Instructions for Playing

Set up a "throne" at the front of the room. Pick (or request) one person to be the king or queen. That person sits on the throne, and everyone else is now designated the subjects.

Have one person facilitate an inquiry, using the following questions to the subjects:
- How would we feel being ruled by this person?
- Would they be a kind ruler?
- A just one?
- Would they be capable of making tough decisions?
- Could they defend the kingdom?

Or, to the ruler:
- You've just been crowned the new king/queen. What do you have to say to your subjects?
- What would you do with your kingdom?
- What would be your first decree?

Facilitator Instructions

Optionally, invite the king or queen to choose advisors, co-rulers, or other roles as desired, and explore why those choices were made and how they fit. You can add your own questions and exploration as well.

Attributions

From the Authentic World Games Night Handbook.

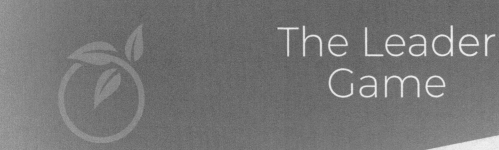

The Leader Game

This is an opportunity to engage with power dynamics, commanding control, making requests, setting context etc.

Instructions for Playing

One person gets to be "Leader", and sits on a higher chair. This person is granted full control of the space for 5-10 minutes.

The Leader makes use of the time in whatever way they want. They might spend the entire time trying to think of what to do, or trying to get consensus from the group, or demanding actions from others. Whatever happens is welcomed and gives us an opportunity to reflect on our experience of being led by this person, and gives the leader an opportunity to see what came up for them when faced with unlimited choice coupled with power.

Attributions

Developed by Amy Silverman of The Connection Movement (NYC).

**Guru Game

Setup
Full Group or
Breakout Groups

Time
20-40 min

This game often leads to the realization that knowledge we seek outside of ourselves is already within; we are gurus to the extent others believe it of us, and normal to the extent that we forget.

Instructions for Playing

One person gets to be "Guru", and sits on a higher chair. Give that person a few moments to get into their "higher self" or "inner guru". The others sit before them and ask questions of the Guru for 5-10 minutes. When done, switch Guru.

This is akin to Hot Seat, but questions are more like, "Oh Guru, what is the meaning of life?" or "Guru, how can I decide when to stay with my lover or when to leave?" The "Guru" is encouraged to fully step into the role of being all-knowing.

Facilitator Instructions

Depending on your instructions and demo, you can make this funny or deep - playful and/or a great way to explore power dynamics and confidence.

Variations

- Guru Panel: Choose 3-4 people to be the gurus. Those people come sit at the front of the group. Anyone can approach, kneel before the gurus, and ask a question. Each of the gurus answers in turn. The penitent can bow and/or say "yes yes yes" and go back into the group. After one or a few questions, switch up the gurus.

- The Guru Of...: Have each guru choose what they are the guru of, for example "The Guru of Love" or "The Guru of Bad Advice", and answer from that persona. BONUS: each guru chooses to be the guru of someone else in the group, and answers as they think that person would!

- Council of the Gods: Designate a line in the room that straddles the worlds of humans and gods. Take a moment for everyone to get in touch with their inner wisdom, then step up to the line as a god. Anyone can step back over into the human world, and ask one question. The facilitator, who straddles the line of god and human, can answer as well as any number of gods.

Attributions

Developed by Authentic World. Variations by the Austin Love Juggernaut and Ethan Sawyer.

Agency and Communion

Setup
Breakout Groups

Time
2 hours

Tools:
1 set of pen and paper
per group

This game is long, but helps to empower self-expression, look at the motivations for our choices, and explore dynamics between the individual and the group. Gifts groups have given include a human couchsurfing chain, silent circles listening to the sounds of nature outside, a "dance virus" party, a ritual welcoming masculine and feminine, and a cozy participant cuddle pile while the facilitators read "Go the Fuck to Sleep."

Instructions for Playing

Break into groups of 4-5. Each breakout group has to decide on a "gift" they want to express to the whole group, such as creating an experience for everybody, offering appreciation, or whatever creative ideas people have!

Take 5 minutes to discuss what you think the group is needing and why. How does each person want the group to feel, or what does each person want to individually feel in the group? Everyone pays attention to where they have shared reality on these desires.

Take another 7 minutes to brainstorm ideas without making a decision. Elect a scribe to write these down. Each member should keep putting their desires on the table, and others practice saying "yes, and..." rather than vetoing or challenging any suggestion (variation: group members can also inquire into why others want the things they want).

Take another 15 minutes for the group to decide on and coordinate a gift using how they want people to feel, and try to create a win/win situation where everybody in the group actually gets something of what they want - in the intention if not the particulars.

End with 5-15 minutes per group to give the gifts.

Facilitator Instructions

Assist with keeping people's attention focused on the objectives for each section of the timed activities (e.g. checking the groups have shared reality on their desires, answering "yes, and..." providing ideas to add or modify other's suggestions, etc.)

Attributions

Sara Ness created this game for an Authentic Leadership Training.

**Block Ops

Setup
Triads

Time
45 min-1 hour

A very powerful way to get traction on stuck spots. I run this on the last day of the Authentic Leadership Training, for my facilitators to work through their fears.

A version of this game is run weekly on the COnnect platform as "Facilitation Fear Lab".

Instructions for Playing

Divide up into triads and choose an A, B, and C. Each person gets 12 minutes to be explored.

A identifies the block that's holding them back most in leadership (or life) right now. B and C propose scenarios that could be done in the moment and might trigger the block.

The group tries a scenario to explore A's block. When the block comes up, A pauses the scenario, and B/C explore what the feelings are in that moment as the block occurs. Alternatively, A can raise a hand when they start feeling their fight/freeze/reaction but continue trying to handle the situation themselves instead of pausing.

Once paused, brainstorm ideas for what A might do in the trigger scenario to have it play out more safely/comfortably. If they have time, they can run the scenario out again with those new strategies. After 13 minutes, take 2 minutes to debrief in the triads, then switch to the next person.

Facilitator Instructions

Facilitator gives time warnings at 5, 10, and 12 minutes; after 5, the triad should be actively in an experiment rather than talking about it.

This game can also be played in a full group of any size. Set up the scenario, then trade out who tries to facilitate it so the group gets multiple examples and tries.

I suggest running this game only with people who have some training or practice in connection or leadership work, as it requires the ability to hold space well for others and also roleplay difficult characters. I usually have 1-3 experienced facilitators wandering the room to make sure that groups are doing okay and actually following the rules of the game - especially trying experiments rather than just talking about them.

Attributions

This game is taken from the Authentic Leadership Training by Sara Ness.

Circling &
IntegralGames

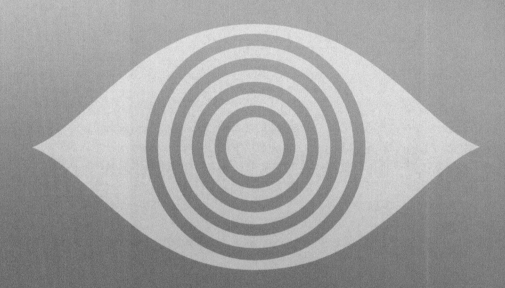

Circling & Integral Games

Circling is probably the most advanced AR game. It's a presence-based conversation focused on unearthing the stories we create about ourselves and others in real time. In circling, time often slows down, deep insights are made, and an almost psychedelic group space of presence can emerge. Talking about it is not enough; Circling must be experienced to be understood.

Circling brings together many of the skills we practice in other AR games, so it works best with experienced participants and a skilled facilitator. However, a solid warm-up series and a few experienced participants can be enough for many groups to get there.

Map of the Territory

· Circling, Dyad Circling, and Spin the Bottle Topical Circling are all variants around the meta-practice of Circling (described in the first game).

· Semi-Circling, Choose-Your-Own-Adventure Circling, and Kabuki Circling are training games for either participating in or leading the practice. Inception and Noticing, in former sections of this manual, are also good lead-in games.

· Guru of the Altitudes and Spiral Sentence Stems allow for an exploration of levels of personal development, corresponding to Integral Theory and Spiral Dynamics..

When to use Circling & Integral Games:

· In training participants for participating in or leading Circling practice
· With experienced AR groups who want to go deeper into relational-level conversation space

Index

· *Circling
· *Choose-Your-Own-Adventure Circling
· Dyad Circling
· *Kabuki Circling

· Spin The Bottle Topical Circling
· Guru of the Altitudes
· Semi-Circling
· Spiral Sentence Stems

**Circling

Setup
Breakout groups
or Full Group (3-10
people)

Time
20 min-whole life.
Average is 45-60 min

Circling is the core practice creating and being created by Authentic Relating. It must be experienced to be understood, ideally many times.

WARNING: Side effects of Circling may include expanded self-awareness, breathtaking perspective shifts, and irrepressible joy. We are not liable for any life-long friendships or relationships that may occur. Circle with care . . .

Instructions for Playing

Circling is a transformational communication practice that enhances self-awareness, creates connection, and teaches participants how to get their needs met AND help others thrive in the process. It is practiced by hundreds of communities across the world.

Part art form, part meditation, part group conversation, Circling has been described as "interactive intimacy", "social intercourse", or (my favorite), "A structured way to love the crap out of someone."

In a circle, you'll join a group of people to have a conversation about what's actually happening for you, and between you, right here and now. You'll get a visceral sense of what others feel, think, and experience around you, and develop a meditation practice for bringing your embodied self naturally out into the world.

Attributions

Experience Circling at **Circle Anywhere** or COnnect Online

Dyad Circling (Wedding Circle)

Setup
Pair / Full Group

Time
45-60 minutes

This game can be used to focus on a tension or issue a couple has in their intimate relationship, two people in a working environment, or any other two individuals who are closely interdependent, particularly on an emotional level. It allows two individuals to dive deeper into issues that may
make one feel stuck and in need of support.

Instructions for Playing

A group of 4–8 people takes place around two individuals who are going to circle with each other.

The dyad only focuses on each other and shares sensations, feelings, imaginations about the other and impacts, like they are Circling.

The people around are putting their attention on the connection between the two individuals in the center and may share what they are experiencing in themselves and the impact that the conversation in the center has on them.

The idea is to really bring the focus on the space in-between the couple and not on the individuals. This should support an environment where none of the people around can take sides for one of the individuals in the middle.

It also supports the dyad to share the experience in their connection without a fear of being judged from the observers around.

Facilitator Instructions

If some people with less Circling experience are involved, it can help if one of the people in the outer circle is taking a leading role. Lead in a way that brings the attention back to connection and the here and now, if the focus gets lost.

Attributions

Brought by Heinz Robert of Circling Switzerland.

Spin the Bottle Topical Circling

Setup
Full Group or Breakout Groups

Time
15 min-2 hours

This is best to play with a group where most or all people have experienced circling before, and has been played with up to 25 participants. It is a creative way to explore a topic while staying in the here-and-now.

Instructions for Playing

Form a circle and place a bottle or other spinnable object into the center. One person spins the bottle. Whoever it lands on gets to choose a topic.

The group then circles with that topic as the focus for 4 minutes. This could involve understanding the topic more, circling different people's relationship to it, or the connection between people around it.

The conversation must be kept relational; if it becomes conceptual, anyone (or everyone) in the group can start making a horizontal circle in the air with their index finger, and the people speaking must bring the conversation back to the present moment.

When the 4 minute bell rings, the person speaking stops immediately or at the end of that sentence, and the person who initially suggested the topic spins the bottle again. Whoever it lands on can choose to either continue the topic at hand, or choose a new one.

Facilitator Instructions

The facilitator may step in to guide the process, as in a normal circle, but the group is often able to self-regulate with the hand signal. The process can continue for any number of rounds. It's a lively, interesting, fun way to create group agency around circling.

Attributions

Organically invented by participants of Authentic Revolution's Boston Circling Training.

Semi-Circling

Setup
Breakout Groups
(6-8 people)

Time
15-30 min

This game is a great way to acclimate and train folks to sustain presence when they are the subject of a group's attention.

Instructions for Playing

The group sits in a semicircle, amphitheater-style, one less chair than the number of people.

One person stands before the group and shares 3-5 felt physical sensations (as in the Noticing game- "I feel [quality of sensation] in my [body location]" describing the nuances or 'flavors' of the sensations itself.

Then, the person shares 3-5 emotions, "I feel [emotion word]." Again, describing the nuances or 'flavors' of the emotion itself. Close, and repeat until each person has gone.

Facilitator Instructions

One way to set up the exercise is by mentioning that stage fright might be defined as "an unwillingness to feel what you're feeling in front of people."

Prompt and invite the person to keep describing just the quality of sensation or emotion, without the 'story' around it.

Try this before Circling or Hot Seat, or to create a sense of group intimacy. This game can take awhile, so time it out accordingly.

Variations

· Shy Variation: If the person standing seems very nervous/fearful, they can start with eyes closed, describing a few sensations. Then have the group close their eyes, and have the person open their eyes, and describe a few more sensations. Lastly, have everyone with eyes open, and the person standing describing some sensations and emotions.

Attributions

From Brian Burrell, of the Houston Authenticity Effect.
Adapted from Sandra Zimmer's workshops on stage fright.

**Choose-Your-Own-Adventure Triads

Setup
Triads

Time
45 minutes

This game can be played with people who are new to circling, and is a great way to practice both tracking and following threads. It can also be used outside of circling as a curiosity-training tool.

Instructions for Playing

Divide the group into triads and choose an A, B, and C.

A is the first circlee. For 2 minutes, A is invited to share about what's on their heart right now.

When the facilitator rings a bell, B and then C each name the thread that most has their attention, whether it be something A said or a way they are being. 1 minute for that. Then A can pick either of those threads to talk about for another 2 minutes.

Repeat the process for at least 2 rounds, with an option for B and C starting to organically pause and name threads to choose if you go for 3 or more rounds (and/or are a more advanced group).

After a few rounds, close by having B and C each take a minute to share what they think they get about A, and then A takes a minute to share what they get about themselves. Switch roles and repeat.

Notes

Invented by Sara Ness for a circling lab.

**Kabuki Circling

"Kabuki" is a kind of Japanese theater known for stylized drama and elaborate make-up. This is one of my absolute favorite games for teaching or introducing circling, or facilitation skills in general. It breaks the practice down into manageable components, helps people identify where they have blind spots and superpowers, and is a fantastic self-realization game as participants see how they tend to show up from what roles do and don't feel natural to them. Be sure to take shares on this one, and invent your own roles to add!

Instructions for Playing

Arrange chairs in a circle. Assign each chair a role, a part of circling facilitation that a participant will take on while he/she sits there. One chair should be designated "The Circlee".

The person in a given chair can use ONLY the tool assigned to that chair during the circle! There is no facilitator, but any participant can speak up at any time in the circle, as they feel called to in their role.

Play for 5-15 minutes. Then, have everybody stand up, rotate one chair to the left, and take on that chair's way of being when they sit. Roles can include:

· The Sensor: Shares bodily and emotional impact ("I feel a wave of warmth rising from my stomach", "hearing that I feel sad," etc.). Can ask the circlee "Is that similar to your experience? What are you feeling?" or other check-in question after sharing.

· The Reflector: Repeats what they heard the circlee saying, without interpretation. Can summarize if they use some of the same words, and can reflect things that particularly hit them.

· The Empath: Listens for what it must be like to be the person being circled. Can try on the body position of the circlee to get more into the circlee's world. Can share, "If I were you, I would be thinking/ feeling/ believing/ experiencing..." or "If I imagine being you..." and then check in to see how it lands.

- The Group Mother: Pays attention to the circle as a whole, noticing if there are people who haven't spoken in a while, who are wearing eye-catching expressions on their face or in their body, noticing how the group as a whole is showing up with the person being circled. Can check in on individuals in the group ("Sensor, I notice you frowning. What's happening for you with [circlee]?"), or share "We seem...with you" to the circlee.

- The Witness: Stays silent throughout the circle, paying total attention to his/her own experience and the experience of being in the circle.

- The Depth Charge: Can ask questions that are relevant to the present moment, and are genuine curiosities. Bonus: Blindfold this person!

- The Romantic: Can state what they are wanting in any given moment.

- The Dissenter: Notices any dissonance that occurs. "You said...but I noticed/felt..."

- The Circlee: Receives the attention and shares their present-moment experience.

- The Body Tracker: Notices and names the physical position and shifts in the circlee.

- The Stud Finder: Speaks the moments they notice the most interest in themself, and when there seems to be most aliveness in the circlee and/or the circle. Can bring things back to where they felt most interest if they feel that the circle is drifting.

- The Time Traveler: Tracks the progress of the circle, can summarize where we've been so far. Can also look for context on how where the circlee is at now fits in with who they are/how they are in life.

- The Truth Seeker: Can speak whatever seems to be an unspoken truth in the moment (In self/other/the circle: a context, a way of being, a tension, a question the circle seems to be skirting around).

- The Speaker for the Moment: Only speaks when the impulse is so strong they have to express, and can't know what they will say before speaking it. They have to speak at least once in the circle!

Facilitator Instructions

Having index cards with the roles written on them placed on the chairs helps in bigger groups. Kabuki Circling can work with groups of any size, although I would suggest that if you have more than 15, run this as a fish bowl with half the people on the outside to watch. This game can also work as general facilitation or leadership training, for any methodology.

Attributions

Invented by Mike Blas of the Austin Love Juggernaut, under the name "Terminator", and was revised by Sara Ness and Chad Phillips.

Guru of the Altitudes

Setup
Breakout Groups

Time
45 min

This is a fun and enlightening game, a great way to help people take on new perspectives and to recognize the wisdom (and partiality) inherent in any single mode of thought.

The most memorable moments, to me, were Jordan (in the Infrared phase) hiding under his chair wrapped in a blanket and hissing whenever he was asked a question - and the elderly psychologist, in the Red chair, who answered the question "What would Jesus do?" with the response, "EAT MY FLESH. DRINK MY BLOOD."

Instructions for Playing

Form groups of 7 or 8.

Assign each chair in the circle a level of development: Infrared (optional if you have fewer members), Magenta, Red, Amber, Orange, Green, or Teal/Integral. Whoever sits in that chair embodies the level of development of that stage, as much as possible - for example, the person in the Amber chair will hold strong traditional values and stand for hierarchy. The person in the last chair gets to ask questions for 4-6 minutes.

Any (or all) of the people in the other chairs can answer the questions, acting as the Guru of their Altitude and embodying the wisdom of that level of development. When time is up, everybody switches one chair to their left, and embodies the next stage.

Attributions

Developed by Jordan Allen and Sara Ness for an Austin Integral meetup.

Spiral Sentence Stems

This game helps bring the philosophy of development into a relatable format.

Instructions for Playing

Get into groups of 4-12 people.

Propose the following sentence steps corresponding to the Altitudes of Development (also known as Spiral Dynamics). Participants answer by either going around the circle to respond or answering popcorn-style, and possibly standing or raising their hands if they resonate with a given answer. Give about 3-5 minutes per stem.

- *(Infrared) My instincts protect me when...*
- *(Magenta) I'm awed by the magical mystery of existence when...*
- *(Red) When I'm free to fully express myself I...*
- *(Amber/Blue) I'm proud to be part of ____ b/c _____*
- *(Orange) I work really hard at...*
- *(Green) When I look inside for truth I...*
- *(Teal/Yellow) Seeing the world as a mirror, I...*

Facilitator Instructions

Read **A Theory of Everything** by Ken Wilber for a more in-depth explanation.

Variations

- Leveled Stems: Participants sit in a circle and take turns completing the stem (about 2 min for each): "As my egocentric self, I think/feel/notice . . . ", "As my ethnocentric self, I think/feel/notice . . . ", "As my world-centric self, I think/feel/notice . . . ", "As my kosmo-centric self, I think/feel/notice . . . ". You can also give a topic to evaluate from each level.

Attributions

Developed by Jordan Myska Allen, former leader of the Austin Integral group and founder of Circle Anywhere.

Games For All Occasions

First date:
- Noticing
- Curiosity
- Google Game
- "One time…"
- Trading Faces (for an edgy option!)
- Sketch Appreciation
- Touch My Elbow
- What I Think You Think of Me
- Context Conversation

Relationship:
- Minis
- Reach Out, Touch Me
- Color Echo
- Next… (go back and forth answering, or answer it every day)
- I Don't Know About You
- Curiosity
- Google Game
- Inception
- Empathy
- "One time…"
- Contexter
- Watermelon
- Complain Game
- Appreciation Dyads
- Sketch Appreciation
- Truths and Withholds (as an ongoing practice)

- NO and Requests Training Game
- Touch My Elbow

Relationship (cont.)
- The Giving Game ("Would You?")
- Context Conversation
- Love and Self-Love
- Rooms of the Heart
- Mirror, Mirror

Work (or work retreat):
- Handshake Game
- Mudra Theater
- Rock, Paper, Scissors
- "How's Yours?"
- I Don't Know About You
- Curiosity
- Google Game
- Hot Seat
- Empathy
- "One time…"
- Appreciation Dyads
- Shower of Love
- Truths and Withholds
- Requests Training Game
- Guru Game
- The Leader Game
- Kingdom
- Core Exploration
- Mirror, Mirror
- Agency and Communion

Edgy Work Games:
- Frustration Station
- What I Think You Think of Me
- Fly On the Wall
  Edgy Work Games (cont.)
- Mirror of Perception
- Constellations

With family/kids:
- Color Echo (esp. Telepathy, Mirroring, or Combo variation)
- Bumblebee
- Group Giving Game ("Would Y'all?")
- Next…
- Whatcha Doin'?
- Word Association
- "How's Yours?"
- "I'm a Tree!"
- I Don't Know About You
- Curiosity
- Google Game
- Spotlight
- Offering Somebody Else's Life As Your Own (The Bollt Blaster)
- "One time…"
- The Love Blaster
- Appreciation Dyads
- Freeze Frame
- The Giving Game ("Would You?")

- Guru Game
- What I Think You Think of Me
- Kingdom
- Love and Self-Love
- "What if..."
- The Lens of Attention
- Constellations

With friends:
- "Frame"
- Noticing
- Bumblebee
- Mudra Theater
- Group Giving Game ("Would Y'all?")
- Whatcha Doin'?
- "How's Yours?"
- "I'm a Tree!"
- Curiosity
- Google Game
- Hot Seat
- Empathy
- "One time..."
- Watermelon
- Complain Game
- Appreciation Dyads
- Freeze Frame
- Shower of Love
- Withholds
- The Giving Game ("Would You?")
- Guru Game
- What I Think You Think of Me

- Fly On the Wall
- Translator
- Context Conversation
- Love and Self-Love
- "What if..."
- Mirror, Mirror
- Imitation Introduction
- Spin the Bottle Topical Circling (if they know circling)

With strangers:
- Noticing
- Curiosity
- Google Game
- Hot Seat
- Empathy
- "One time..."
- Guru Game
- What I Think You Think of Me
- Context Conversation
- The Lens of Attention

For conflict:
- I Don't Know About You (specific to the conflict)
- Curiosity
- Empathy
- Complain Game
- Truths and Withholds
- NO
- "What if..."
- Mirror, Mirror

All:
Sentence Stems
Curiosity
Google Game
Empathy
"One time..

A
R

Games Index

Games Index

AR

Games Index

Other Resources

COnnect
COnnect is an online Authentic Relating and Circling community for those who feel a longing for deeper connection and are looking for a community to practice with. You may continue your journey every day with live, interactive events.

The Authentic Life Course
The ALC is a seven-week-long online turbocharger for personal growth around your relationships and everyday interactions. It has all the tools and accountability you need to actually change the way you interact and show up in your connections.

Facilitation Academy
Facilitation Academy programs are the most comprehensive, material-rich online trainings our students say they've ever encountered. Offered in coached or on-demand versions, and including certification possibilities, the courses contain more than 111 videos by 9 master teachers on all aspects of facilitation and leadership. Useful for beginner facilitators looking to go pro, or professional facilitators who want to expand your authentic skills.

Other Manuals
The AR Games Mini-Manual: A synthesized version of this, good for starting off.

Authentic Relating Aftercare: An integration guide for participants to use after relational events. It defines common terms, explains core values, and troubleshoots situations like the "vulnerability hangover" and what to do if you get authentic and it isn't received well.

Creating Authentic Communities: A guide to starting and running communities around Authentic Relating and Circling practices.

Guide to Getting Worlds: A Circling manual, on the art of understanding others deeply.

Social Technology for the Workplace: A manual developed by **AuthTeams** for increasing connection and trust within companies.

All manuals are available at
www.gumroad.com/authrev

Other resources are listed at
www.authrev.org

AR Adjacent Games

Liberating Structures

Liberating Structures make it easy for leaders of all levels to create conditions for people to work at the top of their intelligence and creativity. In this environment, people thrive and enjoy their work. It is also the path to top performance.

Future Togetherness Test Kitchen

This is a wonderful set of Games that are similar to Authentic Relating, put together by a group over in Europe. I'm loving finding little pockets of social experimentation all over the world. It's rare to have one do such a great write-up of their tools

The School of Life

The School of Life is a global organisation helping people lead more fulfilled lives. They have wonderful tools, physical and therapeutic, for growth in connection and empathy. I particularly recommend their Conversation Menus.

Askhole cards

This is my current favorite question-deck, with questions that range from whimsical to deep to challenging to fun.

Cards for Connection

A beautiful set of cards inspired by Authentic Relating and other practices.

Nonviolent Communication

With NVC we learn to hear our own deeper needs and those of others. Through its emphasis on deep listening—to ourselves as well as others—NVC helps us discover the depth of our own compassion. This language reveals the awareness that all human beings are only trying to honor universal values and needs, every minute, every day.

The Connection Game

110 beautifully designed cards from Ruby May's Connection game, divided into four categories that explore different ways of relating: verbal, physical, play & moments to pause.

Acknowledgements

This manual is the work of nine years (and counting). It contains a multitude of exercises, with the intention to increase presence, connection, self-awareness, and empathy in groups around the world. The "Games" contained here have been extensively play-tested. If you have contributions or variations as you try them out in your own community, please email sara@authrev.com.

Communities and individuals that have contributed to the creation of this manual:

Isaac Cohen, Ali Hussein, Chad Phillips, Jessica Sager, Mike Blas, Becky Kangas, Annabeth Novitski, Megan Rose Browning, Brave Legend Pietri, Micah Sutton, Sharon Swedlow, Kai Koru, Jonathan van Matre, Rob Razmah, Shane Orton, Katie Stellar Dutcher, Scott McClellan, David Staab, Josh Sabik, Sara Ness, Ross Cooper, Sara Katelyn Yeater, Zachary Robison, Emma Joe Anderson, Jeannie Bogue, Ebony Phillips, Ankati Day, Phil Santos Brian Burrell Jordan Myska Allen, David Bollt, Jeffrey Platts, Alexis Shepperd and Shana James, Michael McDonald, Decker Cunov and Bryan Bayer, Guy Sengstock, Robert MacNaughton, Jason Digges, Michael Porcelli, Daniel Johnson, Amy Silverman, Dan Sieling, Rachel Santos, Scott Gregory, Chris Gongaware, Wouter Slegers, Russell Price, Elise Lorraine, Erin Brandt, Ruthie Odom, Peter Will Benjamin, Jennifer E Ott, Abbi Jaffe, Daniel Deterrence Brooks, Patrick Wolf, Valerie Steen, Shaina List, Naveed Heydari (Authentic Denver), Elisabeth Brustein, Rob Hamshar, Indigo Townsend, Telind Bench, Ethan Sawyer, Kim Marie Glynn, Surelys, Galano, Jessie Reilley, David Betz-Zall and Laureli Shimayo, Kip Dooley, Franziska Curran, Dianne Zomper.

Thank you all for your hard work, and your generosity in sharing these games!

Finally - this is, personally, my life's work. Founding communities that make for a more connected and empathic world is my passion, and the aim of Authentic Revolution, the company I co-founded to spread Authentic practices far and wide. If we can help in any way to support the creation and growth of you or your community, please find us at www.authrev.org for individual and team consulting, coaching, or facilitation and leadership trainings.

Happy connecting!

Love,
Sara

Made in the USA
Coppell, TX
24 November 2024